THE NEW MILITANTS

THE NEW MILITANTS

Murzban Jal

THE NEW MILITANTS
Murzban Jal

First Published 2014

ISBN 978-93-5002-262-7

Published by
AAKAR BOOKS
28 E Pocket IV, Mayur Vihar Phase I, Delhi 110 091
Phone : 011 2279 5505 Telefax : 011 2279 5641
info@aakarbooks.com; www.aakarbooks.com

Printed at
Mudrak, 30 A, Patparganj, Delhi 110 091

Acknowledgments

The Thrissur Chalachithra Kendram invited me to deliver the Pavitran Memorial Lecture at Thrissur, Kerala in late January 2013 in connection with the 8th International Film Festival. My thanks to the organizers of this lecture especially Damodar Prasad and Cheriyan Joseph. This little work is an outcome of that lecture. My thanks also to Anjaiah Nannapaneni who asked me to speak on the legacy of Karl Marx a few months prior at the Centre for Scientific Socialism, Acharya Nagarjuna University, Guntur, Andhra Pradesh.

This work was done at the Indian Institute of Education, Pune, one of the few mainstream institutes in India that thinks of education and culture in the socialist perspective. I would like to thank everyone at the institute that made possible this little work.

The New Militants

The New Militants is a rendering of a certain form of Freudo-Marxist dramaturgy where the *Manifesto of the Communist Party* is redrafted on the stage of 21st century history. It is an understanding of revolutions in the era of New Imperialism, an understanding that talks of how the socialist experiment of the 20th century was destroyed by Stalinism. It is thus extremely suspicious of what one calls the "established left" that is caught up in a strange kitsch of Stalinist bureaucracy and parliamentary liberalism. But in this politics of suspicion it unleashes a second suspicion, this time on the tradition of revolutionary adventurism. Principally it argues how Marx's idea of the proletariat is refigured as the revolutionary multitude. Against the old sites that the left operated on, namely civil society and the state, *The New Militants* argues against both civil society and the state. And just as Marx had talked of the "smashing of the state" as the prelude to world revolutions, *The New Militants* works on this theme of anti-state politics based on the young Marx's theme of the "transcendence (*Aufhebung*) of the state" along with the complete transcendence of class societies. Marx's theory of human alienation and fetishism remains at the basis of this dramaturgy.

This stage is set with a number of characters. Because of the mist-enveloped regions of the contemporary bourgeois world, one cannot easily identify the characters of this dramaturgy. What one sees is a ghost reminiscent of Shakespeare's *Hamlet*. This ghost in the age of neo-liberal capitalism is actually the

Nehruvian welfare state that is destroyed by his own brother, Claudius who has taken the form of the contemporary neo-liberal state. A number of characters are seen next to this ghost. Alongside the ghost one notes the presence of Hamlet the original Prince of Denmark appearing sometimes as the Prince of Liberal Democracy and sometimes as the Prince of the Parliamentary Left. Both the ghost and Hamlet seem to be scared. What seems to be scaring the ghost and Hamlet is another ghost, or to be precise, a specter that is humming a tune: "A specter is haunting the world, the specter of communism". Along with this Red Specter are the popes and czars who are busy, both at evoking the Red Specter, as well as busy trying to exorcize it.

With the coming of this Red Specter the mist that covers the stage disappears. A number of characters are seen alongside the ghost of the welfare state, the Red Specter and Hamlet. However, instead of seeing characters from the age of secularism and reason, one notices characters right from the times of biblical creation. We have therefore Monsieur God, the first capitalist and landlord, Adam the first 'man' and also the first proletariat condemned by Monsieur God to toil eternally for the bourgeoisie and Eve the first woman also the first whore condemned by God to be a part of the global sex industry.

Since this dramaturgy is determined by class struggle, the proletariat as the international multitude also enters the scene of history. They try their best to deal with Monsieur God. It is Hamlet the Prince of Liberal Democracy who tries to join the ranks of the proletariat, but seized by existentialist angst he rushes to the parliament thinking that this parliament is the temple of democracy where Monsieur God could be appeased to give up his cruel sadomasochistic ways. This space of existentialist cowardice is filled up by Faust who indeed "takes arms against the sea of troubles" by selling his soul to the devil to challenge the sovereignty of God. If Hamlet is seized by cowardice, Faust is seized by a form of restlessness. He takes to revolutionary terrorism. He shoots at God. God however, though wounded, incarnates himself into the Indian state. This incarnation of the original God then declares Faust a menace and the single biggest threat to Indian security. It is here that the New Militants enter the scene surprising not only Hamlet and Faust, but also Monsieur God, the first capitalist and landlord. Whether God dies in this bloody class struggle and whether humanity can really be liberated thus ending what Marx had once called the "pre-history" of humanity remains to be seen.

The time is out of joint; O cursed spite,
That ever I was born to set it right!

William Shakespeare, *Hamlet*, Act I, Sc V.

Characters:

Claudius: The Neo-liberal State pretending to be very liberal, but in actuality confusing genocide with economic development. While the Indian Neo-liberal State is said to be safely in the hands of the alleged 'secular' party, with the cacophony of the Indian fascists staking claim to complete power in 2014, the state could be no longer safe; just as we are told that in neighboring Pakistan the nukes are safe with the liberals and the American supported generals, but not with the terrorists.

Ghost: The Nehruvian Welfare State that is said to be destroyed by his brother Claudius.

Hamlet: The Prince of Parliamentary Democracy (and the child of Nehruvian democracy) who is tormented by the pretender New Sovereign (Claudius: The Neo-liberal State) and haunted by the ghost of his murdered father. Hamlet is also an existentialist, besides being a parliamentarian. At heart he is a Social Democrat. He cannot stand imperialism and communal-fascism, but can never understand what capitalism is. He thinks that Marxism is a doctrine, in fact a very good doctrine, but has perpetual fear of seizing power.

Faust: He is a misfit in this Shakespearean tragedy. A child of German Romanticism, liberalism of all sorts is alien to him. He has disdain for Claudius, the ghost and Hamlet. Unlike Hamlet he cannot "suffer the slings and arrows of outrageous fortune". Instead he "takes arms against a sea of troubles, and by opposing them" seeks to end them. He is the Master Revolutionary Terrorist, a form of classical Sergey Nechaev. He is also what Marx calls the "alchemist of the revolution".

The New Militants: They have no regard for ghosts or terrorists. They are realists, terrible realists. They have no regard for the bourgeoisie and make no distinction between the liberals, neo-liberals, conservatives, neo-conservatives, fascists, etc. The

New Militants think that all these deserve to exist in the museum of the capitalist mode of production. Above all they are humanists and communist militants. Being realists they face reality directly. "Words, words, words", those words that plagued Hamlet's mind, do not appeal to them. As realists their hands are full of muck. The state hates them, thinks that they are terrorists who need to be eliminated for the sake of national safety. They are the New Untouchables. Being untouchables they know that the Indian caste system is the basis of Indian reality and that modern classes are both inexorably bound to them, as also trapped in them. If they dislike the state for its crass hypocrisy, they also dislike the Brahman comrades. They think that the 10th Mandala of the *Rg Veda* where the notorious caste system was first outlined with the Brahmans depicted as monopolist ideologists backed by the warrior castes as the wielders of the Repressive State Apparatus, while the rest declared as unclean and damned other; is not merely some dead ritual that existed once-upon-a-time in the apparent 'golden' age of imperial 'Hindu' India. They think that this is the foundational myth of the Indian social system that is found not only in the liberal and fascist parties but which somehow has also plagued the established left movement. Being humanists and communist militants they hate all authority, whether economic, political or theological. If they wield their weapons on the state, they will not leave the modern popes and czars.

Though the above are parts of a dramaturgy where Shakespeare's *Hamlet* is replayed in the 21st century with a number of new characters, we start with a trialogue between three real people, Gandhi, Ambedkar and Nehru. This imaginary trialogue is at the same time a very real one. Let us have a look at what they say.

Gandhi: I am the original Machiavelli. I have transcribed his *Prince* into my *Hind Swaraj*. Like the *Prince* my text is a manifesto, but very different from the genre of manifesto penned by Marx and Engels. As in the original Machiavellian text, so too in my manifesto there is a great divide between the multitude and the ideal state that one seeks. My greatest problem has always been that I do not know what to do with both the multitude as well as with this state, but I leave this problem to my friend Mr. Nehru. Recently I have been described as a "conservative democrat", and I think that this description fits in really well. In England in my student days I met the theosophists and learnt how to repackage Tolstoy, Ruskin and the entire repertoire of romantic anti-capitalism into the imaginary called *sanatanadharma*. I believe that Narendra Modi is also some sort of *sanatanadharmist* and theosophist. Philosophers also remember me today. Recently Slavoj Žižek has called me a social-fascist.

Nehru: I am a liberal, also an Aryan son of an Aryan, a discoverer of India and son of a discoverer. One could call me the Christopher Columbus of India. Since there is a Machiavelli in the form of my friend Gandhi, I like to think myself as another type of the Modern Prince, namely Hamlet. And like the original Hamlet I am haunted by a ghost. Quite often I appear as Kerensky and I must say I am extremely lucky since there are no Bolsheviks in India. However, since my own heirs have forgotten me in the name of neo-liberal capitalism, forgotten me for their deep love for the American Empire, I must say that it is my cousin the parliamentary left that should be considered as my most true and honest heir. Once-upon-a-time I played the role of Hamlet. Now it is the turn of the parliamentary left.

Ambedkar: I hate social fascism and I agree with Lenin that the liberals are "civilized hyenas". I am neither Machiavelli nor Hamlet, but since I have to appear on stage, I shall appear as a specter reminiscent of the Red Specter that haunts Old Europe, haunting thus not only the archaic and modern Hamlets, but the entire world of Gandhism, not to forget the worlds of liberal democracy at large. Marx had once said that "traditions of the dead weigh like a nightmare on the brains of the living". It is my endeavor to exorcise these traditions. Since we are dealing with the politics of revolutionary democracy, we must deal with the core problem in India: that of caste and its ideological representation that goes by the fashionable name called "Hinduism". I must remind everyone that "Hindu society is a myth. Hindu society as such does not exist, being only a collection of castes which has no feeling that is affiliated to other castes except when there is a Hindu Muslim riot." But this formulation of "Hindu society" is not merely a myth. 'Hinduism' is a fetish, a signpost of domination and a monster more diabolic than the one conceptualized by Mary Shelley, born firstly from the Brahmanical counterrevolution against Buddhist India, and then reimagined by the Orientalists and institutionalized by the colonial state. And yet we in India seem to be at extreme ease with this fetish. To deal with a truly democratic society one will have to deal with this fetish. That the 2014 national elections are coming up and the minister of genocide dressed up as the minister of development is trying to seize the throne of Delhi, one must stop being liberals, one must as Lenin once said, do "party work in the masses". What we need to say that this old fascist doctrine is not given up by the ones who attempt to seize the throne of Delhi. Consider their macabre words:

> The foreign races in Hindustan must either adopt Hindu culture and language, must hold to respect and hold in reverence Hindu religion, must entertain no idea but those of the glorification of the Hindu religion and lose their separate existence, to merge in the Hindu race, or may stay in the country, wholly subordinated to the Hindu nation, claiming nothing, deserving no privileges, far less any preferential treatment—not even citizen's rights.[1]

To this fascist theory that could be realized in the very near future, I firstly agree with Marx who once said that the critique of religion is the beginning of all critiques. I supplement his radical humanist theory with something very concrete:

> Hindu society seems to me to be in need of a moral regeneration which it is dangerous to postpone. And the question is who can determine and control this moral regeneration? Obviously only those who have undergone an intellectual regeneration and those who are honest enough to have the courage of their convictions born of intellectual emancipation. Judged by this standard the Hindu leaders who count are in my opinion quite unfit for this task.[2]

I completely disagree with those who try to bifurcate the theory of Marx with what I want to say. Instead, I supplement his theory that originated in Germany and thus reframe his theory that all problems emerge from human alienation (*Entfremdung*) and class divided society with my Buddhist inspired idea that sorrows (or *Dukha*) emerge from class society.[3] I am not a postmodernist (like many of my so-called followers) and do not split the question of caste from class. Nor am I trying to create a spiritual theology that would replace Hinduism. Instead, I will become a type of humanist Marxist who relates *Entfremdung* with *Dukha*. This will be my "experiment with truth", and I shall agree with Žižek's idea of the "politics of truth". If Marxism opposes the politics of truth with the "cunningness of the ruling classes", I agree with this wholeheartedly. Let us thus try to understand what this cunningness of the ruling classes is and what a militant Marxism has to say about it. I agree with Marx's formulation of the terrible past yet haunting us:

> Alongside of modern evils, a whole series of inherited evils oppress us, arising from the passive survival of antiquated modes of production, with their inevitable train of social and political anachronisms. We suffer not only from the living, but from the dead. *Le mort saisit le vif! We are seized by the dead!*[4]

This communism, as fully developed naturalism, equals humanism, and as fully developed humanism equals naturalism; it is the genuine resolution of the conflict between humanity and nature and between humanity and humanity.

Karl Marx, *Economic and Philosophic Manuscripts of 1844.*

If democracy, in essence, means the abolition of class domination, then why should not a socialist minister charm the whole bourgeois world by oration on class collaborations? Why should he not remain in the cabinet even after the shooting-down of workers by gendarmes has exposed for the hundredth and thousand times, the real nature of the democratic collaboration of classes?

V.I. Lenin, *What is to be Done?*

This is the point on which one cannot and should not concede today, the actual freedom of thought means the freedom to question the predominant liberal-democratic "post-ideological" consensus—or it means nothing.

Slavoj Žižek, *Lenin's Choice: Interpretation vs. Formalization.*

On the "Cunning of Historical Reason"

Though we did start out with something hovering between the poetic and the prosaic, it must be stated that one will directly have to turn to the scientific. This *Real of the Scientific*—the Real is from Lacan's repertoire, the Real that is different from the Imaginary and the Symbolic—will have to then be directly materialistic and verifiable. We thus start with Marx's discovery of the new continent of knowledge—the continent of history. Though it was Louis Althusser who had made this phrase famous, one will take his theoretical problematic with great reservation. Instead of Althusser's 'structuralist' theoretical anti-humanist idea of history, we talk of Marxism as a theoretical-humanism. We then claim that he indeed discovered a new continent of knowledge, a continent that has reservations of human alienation within it. Two intertwining terrains of scientific knowledge are bound together, history and human alienation.

It is because of this binding of history with alienation (the German term *Entfremdung* could be more meaningful, for it implies an entrance into a very strange and uncanny world), we also claim that history appears as a very dicey character, sometimes appearing in rational form, but quite often than not appearing in the cunning form that Hegel had labeled as "the cunning of reason" (*Die List der Vernunft*). In fact it is this cunning form that Marx had grasped when he had attributed Aristotle's idea that surprise is the beginning of all philosophy.[5] What we find in history is more cunningness and surprises, than simple honesty.

It is with these two perspectives—cunningness and surprise—that we turn to our reflections on historical materialism and how historical materialism needs to become literally a New Physics in Marx's galaxy of knowledge. To understand this it is imperative to understand a complex of contradictory ideas bound to one another:

1. One that cunning and surprise are linked directly to the idea of something terrible, something fearful and morbid causing shock and astonishment. One could derive something from both psychoanalysis and German art theory of the sublime. One needs to go to Fredric Jameson's rendering of the "hysterical sublime" where he talks of "the experience bordering on terror, the fitful glimpse, in astonishment, stupor, and awe of what was so enormous as to crush life altogether... (Here one has) the limits of figuration and the incapacity of the human mind to give representation to such enormous forces."[6] This is also linked to Merleau-Ponty who said that: "The Terror of History culminates in Revolution and History is Terror because there is contingency."[7]
2. The second proposition is from Trotsky: "It is impossible to fool or outwit history. In the long run, history puts everybody in his place."[8]
3. The third idea is Hegel's idea of history as a movement of reason (*Vernunft*) and freedom. Now from all possible Marxists it was Georg Lukács, who is said to have pioneered a form of Hegelian-Marxism in his *History and Class Consciousness*, followed by the once-upon-a-time close colleague of Trotsky, Raya Dunayevskaya, who kept

> this form of Hegelian-Marxism as the basis of her revolutionary philosophy where reason and freedom are intertwined and inexorably bound together that produce the praxis of revolutions.[9] Now it is also known that thinkers who followed her (Kevin Anderson is the best example)[10] kept this Hegelian narrative at the basis of Marx's science of historical materialism and the political practice of world revolutions. Revolutionary Marxism has to be understood as a form of aesthetics, the *aesthetics of freedom*, where we understand the radical "time of the Now"[11], the time for seizing power.

Now what we are doing is combining the element of "cunning" with not only the ideological cunningness of the ruling classes but also something more 'ontological', namely the element of what Marx called the "mystical" in Hegel starting with his *Contribution to the Critique of Hegel's Doctrine of the State*. The mystical is not merely the esoteric blah blahs of religion, or the brutal proclamations of how a minister of genocide can very soon become the Prime Minister of India. Instead this "mystical" that we are trying to relate to the element of the "cunning" is a form of an alienation of humanity where humanity is reified into a monstrous 'thing'. This is what Marx says: In "speculative philosophy reality appears in the reverse (*umgekehrt*)."[12] *Reality appears not as itself, but as another reality.*[13] It is thus a duplicate reality, a form of complete falsity and counterfeit reality. To understand this mysticism, this cunningness and falsity, one will have to go into the deep structures of Marx's reading of Hegelian philosophy combined with his critique of bourgeois political economy.

Now we also know that more than once Marx talked of understanding Hegel as not only the *algebraist of the revolution*, but one who wrote his algebra in the double sites of the rational and the mystical.[14] One could follow Engels who made a distinction between the "dialectical method" (which he considered the rational element) and the "mystical shell" (which he denounced as the conservative part of Hegel.[15] Engels links the mystical with the great burden of theology and the damnation of humanity by the gods, a sort of Germanic, almost

Wagnerian *Götterdämmerung* ("The Twilight of the Gods"). As in Richard Wagner's opera, *Götterdämmerung* or *The Twilight of the Gods*, where destiny, the war of the gods and the apocalypse are the underlying narratives; in the Hegelian mystical the same sort of drama is found.

But what Engels missed out, almost altogether, is that the mystical of Hegelian philosophy (that is bound to the cunning of reason) was linked to the problem of the commodity. This Germanic drama of destiny, the war of the gods and the apocalypse is thus linked to the fetishism of commodities and the secret thereof. And so inexorably was this mystical drama linked to the commodity that Marx said that he was almost forced to quote "the modes of expression peculiar to him (i.e. to Hegel)" when discussing the etiology of the commodity and the theory of value.[16] What happens in this very strange play called *The New Militants* is that Wagner's opera meets Shakespearean tragedy, and this tragic opera then finds realist ground in the real politics in India. Hamlet thus jumps out from the pages of Shakespearean tragedy into politics and appears as advocating parliamentary democracy. His sudden love for the parliament can never be known. But what is most certainly known is that he can never understand what this "phantom commodity" is, how this phantom would be weaving the Shakespearean and Wagnerian arts; and how inexorably this phantom is connected to class society. The tragedy of Hamlet the New Prince of Parliamentary Democracy would be related to the drama of "class society in general" as also with all despotic structures accompanying the ghostly commodity.

Methodologically speaking this mystical drama that carried with it the cunning of history is linked directly to commodity production and the fetishized consciousness produced therewith, where Hamlet like the commodity appears "standing on his head" with his "wooden head" filled with "grotesque ideas".[17] This is the main point that Marx is raising. While its main focus is commodity production, its main 'hope' is utopian socialism that Ernst Bloc outlined in *The Principle of Hope*. Take Bloc's rendering of Maxim Gorky: "It is not enough to portray what exists, it is necessary to think what is wished for and what is possible."[18] But Hamlet with his wooden head cannot think at all, forget think of what is possible. With these grotesque ideas filled in his wooden head he becomes a utopian.

But what does this utopian in thrall of the mystical and the cunningness of history do? The utopian does not think of the necessary and the possible. Instead this utopian, in one of Hamlet's incarnations, constructs a form of justice that is completely estranged from the class structure of society and the property question. This utopian realized as Hamlet talks of humanity in the abstract, talks of "Human Nature" of "Truth" and other metaphysical niceties.[19] This utopian draws "fantastic pictures of future society",[20] pictures drawn of course, from his wooden head. He has "blind belief in the new Gospel". He may not become what Marx and Engels called a "feudal socialist" but he does "stoop to pick up the golden apples dropped from industry, and barters truth, love and honour for traffic in wool, beetroot-sugar and potato spirits".[21] He "endeavors, and that to consistently, to deaden the class struggle and to reconcile class antagonisms."[22] He "dreams of experimental realization of his social utopias, of founding "*phalansteres*," of establishing "Home Colonies", of setting up a "Little Icaria"—duodecimo editions of the New Jerusalem—and to realize all these castles in the air."[23]

It is here that we need to give a very realistic rendering of this tragic opera. We shall turn from Shakespeare and Wagner to real history, in fact real history after the 1917 Bolshevik Revolution. But what happened is that it was not so much Robert Owen and Pierre Proudhon that appear as the creators of this New Jerusalem, but what one can very widely call the "established left" following Lenin's death. Let us thus go thoroughly into this realistic picture. Though the time since Lenin's death was a time of great revolutionary fervor, it was a time when the commodity principle became the basis for almost all types of practicing socialists. The main basis for the cunning of history to operate was the birth of the theory of "commodity-socialism". It was the principle that not only did Stalin keep as the basis of his so-called 'socialist' society in *Economic Problems of Socialism in the USSR* and Mao in his *Critique of Soviet*

Economics, but also which Trotsky and Yevgeni Preobrazhensky placed as a sort of reality that 'socialism' had to live with. That this fetish-commodity would bring in the NEP (New Economy Policy) men and soon destroy the social experiment was something that neither Trotsky, Preobrazhensky, nor Mao took very seriously. One has to note that neither would the so-called experiment of not only commodity-socialism, but also the equally bizarre experiment of socialism in one country would succeed. That Marx and Engels foresaw this double tragedy taking place has also to be noted—"the old filthy business", as they so remarkably said, "would necessarily be restored".[24] It had to be restored. It was restored. The year 1991 was the culmination of this act of great tragedy where Hegel's cunning of reason accompanied by the even more cunning commodity turned the so-called 'socialist' world on its head. It is time that this headless world reads the classics once again:

> Once the commodity-producing society has further developed the value-form, which is inherent in commodities as such, to the money form, various germs still hidden in value break through to the light of day. The first and most essential effect is the generalization of the commodity form. Money forces the commodity form even on the objects which have been produced directly for self-consumption; it drags them into exchange. Thereby the commodity form and money penetrate the internal husbandry of the communities directly associated for production; they break one tie of communion after another, and dissolve the community into a mass of private producers.[25]

It seems the comrades forgot that "*money forces the commodity form even on the objects which have been produced directly for self-consumption; it drags them into exchange, penetrating the internal husbandry of the communities directly associated for production breaking one tie of communion after another, and dissolving the community into a mass of private producers.*" That this human community was dissolved into a mass of private producers was a fact realized not in 1991 but in 1928.

Thus to this element of the cunning of history one also needs to state that after Lenin's death there seemed to produce along with the theory of commodity-socialism a tremendous theoretical crisis, a crisis whereby the world revolutionary movement literally took a backseat. One may also dare say that this form of theoretical crisis stays with us even today, a crisis that produced the New Deal, Stalinism and fascism, besides creating Zionist Israel as the New-fascist state to occupy and police West Asia. But if this crisis did create elements opposing the world revolutionary movement, it also created the a form of 'theoretist' Marxism starting with the Frankfurt School and despite the great theoreticians created (not only following Lenin, but also following Trotsky, Luxemburg, Bukharin, et al) it could not create Revolutionary Marxism. It could create yes Theodor Adorno, Karl Korsch, Erich Fromm, Althusser, the names are just too long, but they did exist only as bourgeois professors, never as revolutionaries. The careful listener will ask: "Why exclude Mao, maybe why even Fidel Castro and Hugo Chavez? And what about the stalwarts within the Indian left movement?" To these one could most certainly answer: "Yes true they are not bourgeois professors, but what impact would they have on the world revolution?" "Would they have the same impact as did Lenin, Luxemburg and Trotsky especially with regard to the questions of revolutionary organization and the makings of the revolutionary party to be precise?"

One thus turns against this form of "academic politics".[26] We do not deal with academic politics, but with Revolutionary Marxism. We desire to turn to what Jacques Lacan calls the "Real", to be precise to the *Real of the Revolution*. We then want a *Revolution with a Revolution*. One knows that it was Robespierre who chided the democrats of the French Revolution who wanted a *Revolution without a Revolution*. The question that we pose is: "How does one reinvent this very radical idea of the *Revolution with a Revolution*?" And will we be morally accountable for this great act?

On Marx's Historical Materialism as a Rigorous Science

Consider our first proposition here. The cunning of history betrayed the "Event of 1917" (as Alain Badiou called it) or the "radical act" (to borrow Herbert Marcuse's term). If the theoretical crisis set in since Lenin's death, it was the Stalin era that concretized this theoretical crisis. Here we would disagree with Žižek who once said that one has "to concede that the rise of Stalinism is the inherent result of the Leninist logic (not the result of some particular external corruptive influence, like the 'Russian backwardness' or the 'Asiatic' ideological stance of the masses)...".[27]

So how does one explain this great tragedy of restoring capitalism in the USSR? And was it actually restored only in 1991 or way back in 1928 where a duplicate socialism pretended to be an authentic Marxism that swore by the name of Marx when in actuality carried out a counterrevolution in the name of Marx? How does one cease repeating these tragedies and farces? To explain this counterrevolutionary tragedy one needs to understand this act of the phantom commodity and how this magical and necromantic commodity (these are Marx's own words) along with its immediate associate "money forces the commodity form even on the objects", we are quoting Engels once again, "which have been produced directly for self-consumption.... dragging them into exchange.... (whereby) the commodity form and money penetrate the internal husbandry of the communities directly associated for production; ....breaking one tie of communion after another, and dissolving the community into a mass of private producers." The simplest answer is to read the good old classics of Marx and Engels, than being foxed by Stalin and Mao. For what they both theorized and practiced was a Revolution without a Revolution, what Marx calls a "crude and thoughtless communism".[28] This Revolution without a Revolution would play the role of the neurotic who would cure his trauma, only to be seized by it once again.

Let us turn to the old textbooks in those 'good' old days of so-called socialism. Recall how the liberals taught us that Marx was so very wrong in talking of socialism taking place in an advanced capitalist country; and how on the contrary the 20th century proved Marx wrong when revolutions occurred in backward Russia and China. What we learnt was that Lenin and Mao were the falsifiers of Marx and these two would then be falsified by global capitalism.

If this was the nursery tale that we were brought up with, the new nursery tale that is being concocted now is how capitalism is unsurpassable, how the American brand of capitalism is the miraculous end of history where the World Bank and the Pentagon would play the Biblical roles of the heavens and the prophets.

So how does one break this myth of the eternal recurrence of global capitalism? How does the radical left re-invent itself? One way would be to pay tribute to Francis Fukuyama who very unwittingly said how the end of history is ushered by liberalism and the "last man" as the fantasized born-again liberal. We pay tribute to Fukuyama because what he unwittingly inferred was that the liberals would not be alone, and that Lenin, Trotsky, Rosa Luxemburg and the entire repertoire of Revolutionary Marxism would once again enter the scene of history. And if the global bourgeoisie thought that they could exorcize the revolutionaries, they were mistaken, for in their inexorable binding to liberalism and capitalism the revolutionaries would return once again.

But in a way one needs also to pay tribute to the Indian state—for recalling the importance of communism—which a few years ago declared one group of the Indian left as the single biggest security threat to the Indian nation. And it is with these two debts that we turn to Marx's understanding of history. Now those who have read Marx seriously may experience a sort of storm and stress between his determinism ("the act just simply had to happen, it was inevitable") and theory of freedom. Take the celebrated 1859 'Preface' to *A Contribution to the Critique of Political Economy* and the 1867 'Preface to the First German Edition' of *Capital* where he is said to talk of "iron necessities".[29] But then also take another case where he says:

> *History* does *nothing*, it 'possesses no immense wealth', it 'wages *no* battles'. It is the *human*, real, living humanity who does all that, who possess all that; 'history', is not, as it were, a person apart, using humanity as a means to achieve *its own* aims; history is *nothing but* human activity pursuing its aims.[30]

So how does one understand this stress if not a contradiction in Marx? What is this play of freedom and necessity? So how does one reconcile the questions of scientific rigour and radical praxis? Can praxis be directly synthesized with a form of what we know as determinism? Or are they completely unrelated?

To answer this it is necessary to move from the realm of Anglo-American philosophizing that we in India are so used to and move to the terrain of Classical German Philosophy. It is necessary to understand that Marxism is not a determinism governed by the rule of the march-past of history that is governed by the fiction of the "iron laws of history". And since Marx does (so it seems at the level of appearance, at least in the 1867 Preface to the first edition of *Capital*, Vol. I) talk of the "natural laws of capitalist production" that work with "iron necessity towards inevitable results" it is necessary to say that this master translation done by Samuel Moore and Edward Aveling under Engels' direction supervision is highly faulty. Marx instead talks of *"eherner Notwendigkeit wirkenden"* where capitalism works, or knits, or even weaves with "brazen necessity".[31] Secondly, the term "inevitable" (or *unvermeidliche*) is not used by Marx (which the English translation shows). Marx never talks of an "inevitable revolution" that is free from revolutionary praxis. Marx instead talks of *"durchsetzenden Tendenzen"* or "forceful tendencies". There is, it seems, the force or compulsion of (and in) history. Thirdly, it must be noted that when Marx used the term "determination" (*Bestimmung*) in his celebrated theorem: the economic base determines the political and ideological superstructure, this term *Bestimmung* ought to be read as "formation" where the economic base is said to form a superstructure.

Now when Marx had introduced the base-superstructure model in his theory of historical materialism, he also inscribed several other models within it. One could differentiate these models as the pure model and the models existing in chaotic form. The model apparently appearing the most at the manifest level of Marx's texts (as well as in the theories and praxis of Revolutionary Marxism) is the pure form model. (We are using the term "pure form" from his *Theories of Surplus Value*, Part I,[32] and the term "chaos" or "chaotic whole" from the *Grundrisse*[33]). By "pure form" Marx means that phenomenon occurs in "typical form", "most free from disturbing influence".[34] But never in the real world does history function solely in manner of this building-like metaphor. Engels' late letter states this problem[35]. The base and the superstructure work in the dynamic relations of dialectical chaos, the economic base stated to be the determining element in the *last resort*.

The whole problem lies when one is not able to understand the deep structures of his scientific revolution. What this science of historical materialism does is that as rigorous science it makes a difference between two sites: (1) the model that appears in *"pure form"*, and (2) the *chaotic model*. The *pure form model* is the model that functions at the *deep level* of scientific inquiry. It operates at the level of everyday life-world in an altogether different way. I call this way of the appearance of the pure form, the chaotic form.

Consequently Marx's theory of history is rigorous, especially his main thesis on the historicity of capitalism which states the inability of capitalism to function when its forces of production have transcended the social structure of society, or in other words transcended its relations of production. This thesis claims (made famous by Marx's in his 'Preface' to his 1859 *A Contribution to the Critique of Political Economy*) that within the base, there occurs a clash between the two levels of the base, i.e. between the forces and relations of production, where the latter become fetters to the development of the productive forces, thus creating havoc in society. Since a clash occurs between the two, one witnesses the transformation in the social structure. In this deep structure, or the pure form, Marx discovers three sites: (1) forces of production (the level of the sciences and technologies), (2) production relations (the structure of society which are comprised of the ownership of means of production and the class struggle), and (3) the ideological superstructure. The former two are the "base" while the third rests on this base. Since quite often there has been a tendency to have a reductionist explanation which gives priority to only the first site (Cohen's explanation in his magnum opus *Karl Marx's Theory of History* is one good example), one must make it clear that the pure form lays only certain methodological guidelines for understanding this new science. In this pure form we see that the movement of terrain 1 (forces of production) to the level of say "A", we also witness the likewise movement of terrain 2 (relations of production) to "A". When terrain 1 (forces of production) becomes "A^1", then terrain 2 (relations of production) likewise follows the same. This, as we insist, operates at the pure form, or the cell form. It is found in the laboratory of historical materialism. Its mode of appearance in the everyday life-world takes an altogether different form. One therefore has to differentiate the cell form from the body form. And that is why we say that this cell form is a "typical form" that is "most free from disturbing influences."[36] Now when one says that there is an inexorable force to move from level 1 to level 2, this is an afterthought, or a scientific thought that operates at the cell form.

The pure form of science shows what Marx calls the "progressive development" of history from primitive communism, via the Asiatic societies, European slave society, feudalism, capitalism, and the consequent struggle for communism. Since there has been a sort of misunderstanding whether Marx implied a unilinear theory of history (made sacrosanct by Stalin) and since Marx's *Ethnological Notebooks* (where he talks of non-European societies and their own concrete course of historical development) has almost been ignored, it must be stated that Marx did not impose a teleological view of history where only the forces of production were seen to determine the development of the course of history. One only has to note Marx's 1877 letter on the Narodniki misinterpretation of history, where he differentiates the concrete analysis of primitive accumulation of capital in Western Europe and the European transition from feudalism to capitalism from what he calls an imposition of this theory onto the whole world, where one has the fantasy of a "historico-philosophico theory of the general development prescribed by fate to all nations".[37] One cannot have, as Marx notes, a "master key" as a "general historico-philosophical theory", for what in the end happens, is being supra-historical.[38]

It is in these spaces of deep structure (the pure form) and the existential structure (the chaotic structure) that we stress

Marx's contribution to the production of scientific knowledge. What one sees, is what one calls after Marx, a "so-called science" which works in a "roundabout way".[39] We call this a *'duplicate' science* because it seems to imitate the scientific method, while in actuality it mimes it in an altogether manipulative way. It is not what one calls "reason", but what we call after the Frankfurt School's use as an "instrumental reason". It uses the "authority of science" while in actuality invoking "magical formulae".[40] This duplicate scientist attempts to be a utopian, but in actuality becomes a *duplicate utopian.*

This duplicate utopian does talk of miracles and miraculous solutions. But this duplicate can never talk of the very basic questions: *"What is humanity?"* and *"How is free humanity possible?"* Consequently if it was said that philosophy is always linked with the sciences[41], then one also says that the sciences (the sciences of the material world) are inexorably linked with philosophy. The world is thus linked to the question: *"How is free humanity possible?"* So if one says that the space that opened is that of the real object as the material for investigation, one now says that science and philosophy are placed under the genre of "critique". What this Marxist science does is place itself as a "critique", a point that not only covers the original Kantian concern of the analysis of the conditions of knowledge, but primarily deals with the analysis of human emancipation. Marxist science deals thus with human emancipation. It becomes "scientific dialectics" as Marx called it, that is derived "from a critical knowledge of the historical movement which itself produces the material conditions of emancipation."[42]

And that is why we insist that by Marx's science, we by no means imply a form of scientism or positivism where a discourse of iron laws of history would displace Marx's critical humanism. And since Marx's original terms seem to be forgotten for the ideology of the marchpast of history, one needs to recall Marx's own idea of the "*human* natural science" or a "*natural science of humanity*"[43] which as "communism is at once *real* and directly bent on *action.*"[44] We thus turn directly to a form of radical praxis that breaks the aura of reification of the marchpast of estranged history. We turn to the *Real of the Revolution.*

To turn to this very radical act one also de-reifies the idea of repetitive history, of history repeating as tragedies and farces to that of revolutionary joy. And it this revolutionary joy that produces what Žižek once called "the sublime feeling of enthusiasm."[45] This sublime feeling finds not the spaces of civil society and the state for the left to operate on, but the space of the "commons" (*Gemeinwesen*). If however the commons is the space that is found in modern capitalism (albeit in a very reified way; Marx here calls it the *Gemeinsame* which destroys humanity and produces monstrous things and ghosts), the Indian caste system that is essentially based on the space of hierarchy and which abhors equality, liberty and fraternity would have to create even more ugly types of monstrous things and ghosts.

One turns now to the caste question. One sees how they are "completely independent idyllic republics" based on the "solid foundation of Asiatic despotism".[46] The 10th Mandala will continue to speak:

> The Brāhman was his mouth, of both his
> arms was the Rājanya made.
> His thighs became the Vaiśya, from his
> feet the Śūdra was produced.[47]

Caste here is not understood merely as primitive division of labour (this was D.D. Kosambi's view[48]), but is something more complex, that combines the issues of class, race and neurosis-psychosis. It is also linked to Marx's problematic of alienation. How the linking of caste with modern classes, thus the linking of caste with industrial capitalism and the global accumulation of capital is done, remains the leitmotiv of this work. The relation between social hierarchies and graded inequality (the sine qua non of the caste system and the philosophy of 'Hinduism'[49]) on the one hand, and the very Marxist issue of class struggle especially the bourgeois/proletariat opposition on the other hand will be studied. Alongside the question of caste and class emerges another issue that of caste and race. We thus pose the question: "Is caste and casteism similar to racism, if not a European type of racism, then at least a South Asian type?" Finally, the problem of caste is also related to the psychoanalytic problem of neurosis and psychosis. It is keeping these three problematic: (1) class, (2) race and racism[50], and (3) neurosis and psychosis that we shall try to locate the question of caste. Combined with these three problematic, one has to deliberate on the question of social and political power in India.

Caste and Religious Fascism in India

To turn to the question of the New Militants that produce this sublime feeling of enthusiasm (the feeling of the "*commons*", of humanity understanding itself as humanity) where the actuality of the revolution finds its real place in history, one needs to go directly into the question of how real democratic philosophy becomes a theory that grips the *masses*. Let me be frank once again. The idea of a democratic mass can never be actualized if the deep-seated structures of graded inequality and the division of labourers (both being the sine qua non of the Indian caste system as Ambedkar so rightly put it) based on hierarchies are not destroyed. This active destruction, this tremendous cultural revolution—where humanity can proclaim its humaneness—is the prerequisite of the communist revolution. It seems that the tragedy of the Indian democratic movement has been the splitting of the caste and the class question. One could fault works like Ranganayayamma's *For the Solution of the 'Caste' Question, Buddha is Not Enough, Ambedkar is Not Enough Either, Marx is a Must* which seem to completely misunderstand Marx's idea of human emancipation that he outlined in *On the Jewish Question* as also forget Marx's complex idea of history, along with his theory that in the Indian variant of the Asiatic mode of production, caste was the economic basis, if not to borrow two Hegelian terms the "essence" (*Wesen*) and the "concept" (*Begriff*) of Indian society itself.

In contrast to these very stale and uninspiring ideas let us turn to Trotsky who conceptualized the Asiatic character of Russian society:

> In Europe 5.4 million square kilometers, in Asia 17.5 million, and a population of 150 million. *In this enormous area, all stages of human development: from the primitive savagery of the northern forests, where men eat raw fish and worship trees, to the most modern social relations of the capitalist city* (my emphasis), where the Socialist worker

> regards himself as an active participant in world politics... *The most concentrated industry in Europe, based on the most backward agriculture in Europe* (my emphasis). The most colossal government in the world, using all the achievements of technical progress of its own country. This is the soil on which social classes, grow, live and fight.[51]

One here has to see Marx's historical materialism in a new light where his much ignored *Ethnological Notebooks* along with the 1881 draft letter to Vera Zasulich is taken into account. It is thus not in the old framework of the unilinear theory of history (where history was seen marching from primitive communism via slave society, feudalism and capitalism and culminating very mysteriously into socialism), but as multilinear history where Marx's Asiatic mode of production is taken for rigorous analysis with the critique of caste taken as its epistemic basis. In this perspective not only would the political principles laid down by all communist parties in India be off this mark, but also the great historians like R.S. Sharma and Irfan Habib would be proved wrong in articulating an "Indian feudalism".

I will begin here with the recent death of a not so-recent fascist in Mumbai the founder of the Shiv Sena and how the Indian liberal moaned at his not so tragic death. We heard from the liberal that this fascist was a "very liberal and tolerant man". Earlier we had heard of a difference between the liberal and the fascist, we heard of the debates in the 1920s and 30s on the relation between social democracy and fascism. Now we hear that the fascist has somehow evolved into a liberal. The old fascist story of racial superiority, caste domination and the totalitarian managerial state remains at the background. Behind this form of fascism that the RSS preaches is also a form of fascism that is not only barbaric with its own citizens, but outrightly imperialist:

> Hinduism, once, used to extend over what is now Afghanistan, over Java, over Cambodia. Powerful Hindu India could reconquer these lands and give them back the pride of their Indian civilization. She could make Greater India once more a cultural reality, and a political one too.... She could teach the fallen Aryans of the West the meaning of their forgotten paganism; she could

> rebuild the cults of Nature, the cults of Youth and Strength, wherever they have been destroyed; she could achieve on a world-scale what Emperor Julian tried to do. And the victorious Hindus could erect a statue to Julian, somewhere in conquered Europe, on the border of the sea; a statue with an inscription, both in Sanskrit and in Greek: What thou hast dreamt, we have achieved.[52]

There are two parts to this narrative of fascism in India. Either locate this as a superstructure emerging only in the ages of capitalism and colonialism, or one has also to see the pre-history of modern fascism in India that had its seeds laid out in Brahmanical Hinduism. The tragedy of India is not only does it have the caste-based society with its "whole series of inherited evils oppressing us" to borrow Marx's phrase, but also that the alternative subaltern histories have not been ascribed in the active memories of the popular classes. Contextualizing the politics of Leninism implies a creation of a radical archive of the subaltern masses. "Leninism" implies this radical humanism, what in the subaltern Marathi tradition is called "*Manuski*" that is in direct opposition to the elite-driven schizophrenic tradition of Brahmanical domination.

In this sense we talk of not only the radical tradition of humanism as opposed to casteism, also called "Brahmanism", that is then reified into the 'innocent' genre called "Hinduism". We talk thus of authenticity of what Lenin called "concrete analysis of concrete conditions", where he does not involve a form of economic reductionism but instead talks of "all aspects of life" and "all classes, strata, and groups of the population"[53]. Authenticity seeks truth and in doing so rebels. It creates a counter-tradition to the orthodox tradition, not merely as opposing tradition, but creates a "tradition that opposes".[54] Its vantage point is found in the philosophy of Phule and Ambedkar. The critique is on caste-Hinduism and also on the fact that modern Indian liberalism did not take the programme of the annihilation of caste seriously, sometimes like Gandhi valorizing it and sometimes like the Nehruvian liberals sweeping it beneath the mystical Indian carpet.

Consider the morality of this caste system where hell is prescribed for the "family destroyers through caste admixture, for, their ancestors fall deprived of mane cakes and libations".[55] Here there could be no better thinker than Ambedkar to understand both the moral crisis of the Indian ruling classes as well as the question of Indian fascism. That this form of Indian fascism is directly supported by the liberals as well as by the international fascist movement has to be noted. Andres Brevik (the butcher of Norway) is a case to be noted. One must also note that Heinrich Himmler (Hitler's notorious deputy) was an avid reader of the Vedas. That there is a similarity between not only the RSS and the European fascists, but also between caste Hinduism (there is nothing called "casteless Hinduism") and fascism has to be understood. Himmler, this *Reichsführer* of Nazism, had founded the *Ahnenerbe* ("ancestral heritage") modeled on the Indian caste system led by the Vedic warrior castes. What is also not much known is that Himmler always carried the *Gita* and took inspiration from it. It is also said that he considered Hitler the reincarnation of Krishna, and he the incarnation of Arjuna. That Ambedkar considered the *Gita* to be an extremely immoral text whose sole politics was the justification of the caste system and war has to be seen in the light of the threat that Indian fascism led by the RSS poses to the survival of secularism and democracy in India. If this so-called 'mystical' east fascinated the Nazis, it now fascinates the neo-fascists. Brevik's *2083–The Declaration of Independence in Europe* is based on this same macabre tradition. And if Nazism was based on this 'Aryan'/'Semite' mythical war, then the RSS takes this fascist theme lock, stock and barrel, and then links it with the contemporary American imperialist theme of the "clash of civilizations".

If one part of Hinduism is outrightly fascist, the other more 'innocent' one seems to be psychotic, in the sense refuses to engage reality. Gandhi represented this trend. Note the leitmotiv of esoteric Hinduism—nature, or rather reality, is an illusion (*maya*). If for Marx, the beginning of all critiques is the critique of religion,[56] then for the Indian left, this state of psychotic denial of the world that Hindu religion keeps at its basis will have to be the beginning of all critiques. The critique of religion, psychosis and capitalism coincide. But it is not only the critique of religion as psychosis—as a "total withdrawal from reality", as Freud's classical definition goes—that one needs to undertake. It is the critique of political theology, or religion that serves the need of fascism and imperialism, that one needs to undertake. We are now no longer in the safe lands of innocence quoting Ashis Nandy's 'An Anti-Secular Manifesto'[57], or debating on the so-called *sanatani* character of Hinduism with the Orientalists. What happens now is collaboration between European neo-right intellectuals and the Indian fascists. Consider the right wing Belgium indologist and ideologist of the RSS, Koenraad Elst. Not only does one have to recall his *Decolonizing the Hindu Mind*, *Who is a Hindu*, *The Saffron Swastika: The Notion of Hindu 'Fascism'*, but even his even more notorious *Ram Janmabhoomi vs. Babri Masjid: A Case Study in Hindu Muslim Conflict*. One has to point out how these "Hindu" texts that are produced in Europe have also an organic connection with people like L.K. Advani. One has to recall the intrinsic connection between European thinkers like himself (along with Francis Gautier) who give intellectual cannon fodder to the Indian fascists. Hinduism has ceased to exist in the genre of Gnostic philosophizing and neo-Platonism that influenced the theosophists, Coomaraswamy, René Guénon and Gandhi. It has become essentially political of a fascist nature. And with Andres Breivik around, along with the threat posed by the RSS in the next general elections of 2014, one knows the magnitude of this problem.

So then what is to be done? If one talks of communist militancy as a form of humanism and naturalism and the aesthetics of insurrection, then how is this politics of direct action to be realized? For this one has to understand the theme of *repeating history*, especially the Leninist variant of *repeating history*. In this theme of repeating history we turn to the problem of identifying caste in India, especially in identifying the genealogy of caste, as also understand the relation between caste in modern neo-liberal India and Indian fascism. The great tragedy of Indian history shall be inexorably linked with the caste question. Central to this theme of caste is the question of capitalism and modern classes and whether the new capitalist structures are able to erase the earlier caste-based mode of discrimination. If tragedy is linked to the genealogy of caste, farce is related to the question of the persistence of caste in the age of modernity. And since the minister of genocide is set to proclaim himself to be the next Prime Minister, one may have to remind him of the:

> ....idyllic village communities, inoffensive though they may appear, (which) had always been the solid foundation of Oriental Despotism, that they had restrained the human mind within the smallest compass, making it the unresisting tool of superstition, enslaving it beneath traditional rules, depriving it of all grandeur and historical energies. We must not forget that the barbarian egotism which, concentrating on some miserable piece of land, had quietly witnessed the ruin of empires, the perpetuation of unspeakable cruelties, the massacre of the population of large towns, with no other consideration bestowed upon them than on natural events, itself the helpless prey of any aggressor who deigned to notice it at all. We must not forget that this undignified, stagnatory, and vegetative life, that this passive sort of existence evoked on the one part, in contradistinction, wild, aimless, unbounded forces of destruction and rendered murder itself a religious rite in Hindustan. We must not forget that these little communities were contaminated by caste and slavery, that they subjugated humanity to external circumstances instead of elevating humanity to be the sovereign of circustances, that they transformed a self-developing social state into never changing natural destiny, and thus brought about a brutalizing worship of nature, exhibiting its degradation in the fact that humanity, the sovereign of nature, fell down on his knees in adoration of Hanuman the monkey, and Sabbala, the cow.[58]

One could say that falling before Hanuman the monkey, and Sabbala, the cow may be fine despite abhorring humanity; but never bowing before the new monkeys and cows of neo-liberal communal-fascism. Somewhere I had talked of how the fact that these 'offensive' passages of Marx correspond to those of Phule and Ambedkar seems to be forgotten.[59] I had also talked of Aijaz Ahmad who had said that "Marx's denunciation of pre-colonial society in India is no more stringent than his denunciation of Europe's own feudal past, or of the Absolutist monarchies, or of the German burghers; his essays on Germany are every bit nasty".[60] Remember that for Ahmad, Marx visualized the power of the caste system in the Indian village—"restraining the human mind within the smallest compass" equals his critique of "the idiocy of rural life" in feudal Europe.[61] Further, for Ahmad, Marx "regarded the caste system as an altogether inhuman one—a 'diabolical contrivance to suppress and enslave humanity', as Ambedkar put it in the preface to *The Untouchables*—that degrades and saps the Indian peasantry, not to speak of the 'untouchable' menial castes."[62] Our emphasis is on the linking of caste with the generic idea of the Asiatic mode of production and that of the infamous Oriental despot.

And here it is imperative to emphasize that the Asiatic mode is a complex genre and cannot be reduced to a Unitarian mode of production. In Iran it takes a certain kind of form, while in China and India it takes different forms. In India it is caste and the peculiar type of social stratification that forms the basis of the critique of political economy of India. In the Indian variant of the Asiatic mode we put caste (and not class devoid of caste) as central to a Marxist radical imagination of historization and humanization of Indian society. We not only recall, but also emphasize Marx's statement that caste has been "the solid foundation of Oriental despotism"[63], celebrating the "wild aimless, unbounded forces of destruction"[64], based on "a sort of equilibrium, resulting from a general repulsion and constitutional exclusiveness, resulting between all its members"[65]. Not only is it the foundation of what I insist on calling "Oriental despotism", it is also the solid foundation of the "inherited evils"[66] that yet possess and haunt modern India. That is why it is pertinent to say that in contrast to the liberal's forgetfulness of caste (Gandhi and Nehru are only two examples), as well as in contrast to the established left that has made a fetish of class (here one means that only modern economic class matters—in fact a European idea of class—and nothing else) and thus ignored the dialectic of caste and class, one needs keeping this dialectic central in order to understand how actual class formations and state power come into the scene of revolutionary history.

One also needs to tell the established Indian left, who seem not to have read Marx critically, that by "modes of production" Marx means something much more profound than what the economist inspired left imagines it to be so. Consider Marx: "Religion, family, state, law, morality, science, art, etc., are only *particular* modes of production, and fall under its general law (i.e. the law of estrangement, private property and the production of reified consciousness. My insertion: M. J.)."[67] One also needs to inform this same "Marx-less leftist" that Lenin had based his revolutionary politics on the radical critique of economism. Taking this into consideration, as also taking into consideration that caste like religion, family, state, law, morality are all modes of production, we insert caste as not only some aberration of Indian society, but as a well-defined social structure, so deep-rooted that we insist on calling it, after Hegel, as the essence or the *Wesen* of social being. In Hegelian terms, caste is understood as the essence, the concept as well as the "Idea" of Indian society.

Reviewing Caste

There are three basic fault lines centralized on the mechanism of caste:

(1) Caste as the alienated "cutting off" of one human from the other governed by the dictatorship of the upper castes. Marx's concept of alienation or *Entfremdung*, where people are compelled to live in a dehumanized and neurotic world, shall be the guiding principle of our analysis of caste. The main theme of alienation where the "loss of the human self" is central, finds a place in our analysis of caste. This human alienation is realized as the dictatorship of the upper castes. This dictatorship is carried out through not only the upper caste panchayats and communal organizations, but also through the medium of the family, the media and other liberal institutions like the parliament and the bureaucracy. Caste is thus not merely related to pre-capitalist rural India, not only related to anti-democratic movements of primordial nativism (best emphasized by the RSS and the Shiv Sena) whereby the Indian right-wing produces a fantasy world that is built on the dream-images of imperialist

barbarism. It is an essential part of the liberal project institutionalized since the early 1920s where the upper caste ideology of the Hindu reform movement sank deep into national consciousness. We will keep Žižek's recent account of Gandhi as a "social fascist" and Jaffrelot's reading of Indian democracy as "conservative democracy"[68] and Gandhi as the source of Congress conservatism[69] that despite its cosmopolitan appearance remains conservative in actual practice. As Ambedkar said Gandhism is a "call of return to Antiquity" as well as a "reanimation of India's dread, dying past".[70] It is this conservative character that the Indian liberals nurtured, thus disabling the program of the annihilation of the caste system.

(2) How the caste system, albeit radically modified in the age of late imperialism in permanent crises, structures minorities like the Muslims along with the traditionally oppressed castes to look like the "hellish other" (to borrow Sartre's term from a different context) that serves the interests of anti-democratic, anti-secular and pro-imperialist forces, and

(3) Caste to be understood as the Confucian lethargy of Indian civilization which serves the production of the political economy of the capitalism-at-the-periphery, as well as the creation of a sluggish de-politicized and fragmented working class that is so internally divided that it cannot play out its role as the insurrectionist proletariat. Here we relate the problem of caste with R.D. Lang's theory of the divided self and Theodor Adorno's theory of the general regression of thinking.

Keeping the above in mind I state that by caste one means *inherited class status* (or *frozen classes*, classes that are involved in the production of surplus, as also classes that are reified and hypostasized) based on segregation that is sanctioned on religious grounds and built on the ideas of purity and pollution.[71] 'Exclusion', one must note is not a transcendental form of exclusion, but exclusion based on concrete political economy. For instance, Irfan Habib mentions that the hunters (the Chandalas and the Nisadas) "were the original untouchable castes.... (who) were excluded from taking to agriculture".[72] Exclusion is thus based in concrete social situations, in concrete political economies.

In this historical materialist model based on the critique of political economy it is the upper castes led by the priestly castes (the Brahmans) accompanied by the warrior clans[73] which are considered 'pure', while the working masses (the Śūdras) are said to be 'impure'. What happens in ancient India despite Buddhism (unlike in ancient Iran, for instance, where Zarathushtra as the messianic prophet of ancient Iran denounced this warrior-priests combine), is that the warrior-priests combine (with the help of the Vedic rituals) could institutionalize this form of domination.

A small note on the term "caste" is necessary. Despite the terms "varna" and "jati' being part of the Indian lexicography, the modern term "caste" is precise to define its characteristic. The word "caste" is itself derived from the Latin *castus* meaning "pure, segregated, cut off", and is etymologically related to *carere* "to cut off".[74] If then caste implies the logic of "cutting off", it gets to be directly related to alienation. One will need to point out the relation between alienation as *Entfremdung* that arouses the feeling of loneliness and helplessness with Freud's concept of *Unheimlich* or the "uncanny" that raises the feeling of dread and terror. And since caste as human alienation and the feeling of the uncanny has within it the discourse of race, the problem of racism inherent in Hinduism is repeatedly raised. Now what seems to be mere cultural criticism from a radical secularist perspective turns into the core question of locating revolutionary subject positions in India. Would caste imply race, and if so would the problem of the political economy of India conjoin the class question with that of caste? In this sense would the 'high' castes, the priests (Brahmans), the warriors (Kshatriyas) and merchants (Vaiśyas) be considered part of the ruling establishment and the Śūdras and ati-Śūdras be understood as the proletariat? Then is caste=class and class=caste and that at both the levels of the ideological superstructure and the economic base one has to unleash a cultural revolutionary attack on Hinduism? Would this attack be the prelude to the critique of political economy in India? In this perspective of the caste-class combine, one must also note that while caste remains a part of the history of India in particular, caste takes a more generic form, where understood as an oppressive social system, was also linked to the Asiatic states and even to the counterrevolutionary bureaucratic Stalinist state.[75]

A small note on the origins of caste is necessary. Since social science has attempted to locate a manifold origin of caste: from the Indo-Iranian origins to the period from the rise of Buddhism to the Gupta period[76], its genealogy and structural analysis is necessary. The scientific point of view locates caste in the complex of social formations that is itself based on a form of labour process that produces surplus.[77] Removing caste from this space of historical social formations would only make the reading of the caste question extremely unscientific. Secondly attempting to locate caste exclusively as a conspiracy created by a specific social group could be erroneous. Caste is so unfortunately deeply rooted in Indian civilization and intrinsically woven in India's social fabric (and that though it is represented both theologically and ideologically in Hinduism) its encounter with Buddhism and then with Islam and Christianity did not allow the uprooting of this system. It seems that despite Buddhism's humanist and anti-Vedic worldview and despite Islam's egalitarianism, the Buddhist and Muslim rulers not only did not challenge it, but used it for their own advantage. Irfan Habib, for instance, claims that not only in Brahmanism, but also in the times of Buddhism and Islam, caste was present.[78] The sources drawn by Habib will be of great help, though as we shall see, he does not want to link it with the Asiatic mode. Not only does he link caste with Brahmanism and Buddhism, but also with the Islamic rulers[79], despite both Buddhism and Islam's ideology of egalitarianism.

How does one understand this irony that despite anti-caste religious ideologies (in Buddhist and Islamic times), caste continuously persisted in Indian history? How does one understand that it is not created by some sort of idealist conspiracy independent of the questions of land, labour and capital, but located in a particular social formation? But also how does one understand how in almost similar social formations (existing in India and Iran in medieval times) in one case (India) caste was prominently present, and in the other

(Iran) it did not prevail?[80] Would then, the Iranian version of the Asiatic mode of production give way to different results, which do not correspond to the Indian variant?

Linking caste to the question of the Asiatic mode of production also brings in the question of human geography as well as the very important issue of origins into our discussion. One will have to turn one's attention to ontogenesis and phylogenesis. The origins of caste are complex and diverse ranging from the versions given from Kosambi to Habib and from Georges Dumezil to Gherardo Gnoli. Historical analysis traces the domination of the Indo-Iranian military elites (the Indian *Kshatriyas* and the Iranian *Rathaēštars* (literally "the wielders of the chariot") in the Late Bronze Age with discovery of bronze and production of the chariot as the vehicle for raiding pastoral communities. According to Gnoli the primary class struggle was between these warrior tribes (the Indian *Kshatriyas* and the Iranian *Rathaēštars*) and the agriculturalists (the Indian *Vaiśyas* and the Iranian *Vastryō.fśuyants*).[81]

To understand this class struggle in the ancient Indo-Iranian world whereby one understands the origins of caste, one needs to understand how the Indo-Iranian warrior-priests combine could dominate the agriculturalists and the pastoral communities through the ideology-ritual of Yagna. Yagna was not merely a religious ritual. It was a mode of destruction of the surplus produced by the agriculturalists and the pastoral communities. One needs to stress the theory of trifunctional ideology as introduced by Dumezil in 1929 where proto-Indo-European society was divided into three classes: the priests, warriors and the working multitude (the farmers, herders, craftspeople and traders). What happened is that corresponding to these three ancient classes were the three great economic activities: the sacred/political (dealing with the ideology and practice of sovereignty—this is the Ideological State Apparatus), war/defence/policing and internal repression (the Repressive State Apparatus) and economic production. While in a certain way historical materialism would state that there is a shared code between the Indians, Iranians, Romans, Greeks and Germans with this tripartite division of society, what happened in the Indian subcontinent is that these three classes got reified into castes with its corresponding theological sanction, while also producing the "great refusal" (to use Herbert Marcuse's term from a different context) in the form of the Śūdra and the ati-Śūdra communities. The fact that there is a genetic affinity between the upper castes in South Asia with Europeans, while the lower castes are more like Asians has to be pointed out. A 2001 study pointing to these conclusions also highlights Phule's thesis of the upper caste elites being parts of the European stock and thus Indo-Iranian raider tribes, where stratification according to the principle of racial colour (*varna*) was the basis of their class rule.

Here one needs to go to Albêrûnî who points to this race-based classification regarding the Indian castes. In his chapter 'On the Castes, called "Colours" (Varna), and on the Classes below them', in his magnum opus *India,* Albêrûnî talks of the apparent 'genius' of the kings of ages gone by who invented the caste system to prevent the 'disorder' of intermixture.[82] Iranian mythology claims that Jamshid (in Middle Persian), who appears as Yima (in Old Persian) and Yama (in Old Sanskrit) created class divisions. The *Sháhnáma* (the eleventh century Persian classic penned by the legendary Firdausi) says that Jamshid created the four *Anjuman* (literally "institutions" or "assemblies").[83] This is how the rendering goes. Note the origins of institutions of pre-capitalist class formation in Iranian literature. Remember that the Persian words are *Anjuman* and *Guroh* implying "assembly", "congregation", "troop" and "band". How it is related to caste as a pre-capitalist institution and whether it is related to the Hindu order based on purity and pollution where untouchability remains the essence of its system remains to be seen:

> Then to the joy of all he founded castes
> For every craft; it took him fifty years,
> Distinguishing one caste as sacerdotal
> To be employed in sacred offices,
> He separated it from other folk
> And made its place of service on the mountains
> That God might be adorned in quietude.

Arrayed for battle on the other hand
Were those who formed the military caste;
They were the lion-men inured to war—
The lights of armies and of the provinces—
Whose office was to guard the royal throne
And vindicate the nation's name for valour.
The third caste was the agricultural,
All independent tillers of the soil,
The sowers and the reapers—men whom none
Upbraideth when they eat. Though clothed in rags,
The weavers are not slaves, and sounds of chiding
Reach not their years. They are freemen and labour
Upon the safe soil from dispute and contest.
What said the noble man and eloquent?
"'Tis idleness that maketh freemen slaves".
The fourth caste was the artizens. They live
By doing handicraft—a turbulent crew
Who being always busied with their craft
Are given much to thought.[84]

Whilst the origin of the Indian and Iranian history has a family resemblance, both histories after the separation of these tribes sharply demarcate. The character Jamshid is the common person, appearing as Yama in Sanskrit and Yima in Persian. Jamshid (in Iranian legend) not only creates classes. He also creates endogamy and the consanguine family system. Note that this consanguine family system is the essence of Hinduism and the caste system. The irony is that this legendary Indo-Iranian hero appears as both hero and sinner.[85] This sin or crime is not mentioned. It seems that, if one brings in Marx, that he becomes a criminal in creating classes. For Freud, his crime is that he institutionalizes incest. In the *Rg Veda* he also appears as a fallen hero but for exactly opposite reasons, for he refuses to have sex with his sister Yami.[86] He then does not create endogamy, or if he does, is also responsible for breaking it.

It is important to note that while this legendary criminal-hero (the Iranian Faust: he is a fallen prophet, a prophet who refuses to believe in god according to the *Avesta*) creates the class division; in India it is Manu who is the inventor of this absolutely dubious institution of caste stratification. If Jamshid could become part of the romantic Iranian poetic tradition (by refusing to believe in god), in India Manu could only be a criminal devoid of any heroic-poetic significance.

Since the Ur-origin of caste is related definitely to the Rg Vedic tradition, one has to understand its relation to the Indo-Iranian past. We saw how in the Hindu caste system the alienated cutting off one social group from another is the sine qua non of India. But see the above Iranian narrative. There is class stratification, but this is not the same as caste stratification as in the Hindu-Brahmanical model based on the totem of purity and the taboo of pollution. Remember that however brutal the Iranian mode of Asiatic pre-capitalist social formation was (which reached its epitome in the late Sasanian era, probably in the late 5th century A.D.), it did not take in this peculiar form that emerged in India. The reason? One could say that a form of human geography that forms a part of historical materialism could be the basis. It must be noted that though the Indo-European model that we just mentioned formed a type of a generic model of class formations that was common with the Greeks, Romans, Iranians and the Indians; there is a considerable difference between the Greco-Roman model on the one hand and the Indo-Iranian on the other, not to forget a difference between the Iranian and the Indian type of class formation. To explicate the latter point it must be noted that in Iranian tradition the king of kings (*Shāhān Shāh-ī-Ērān*) was a messianic form of personification of all the classes. He was priest, warrior, peasant and artisan all at the same time.

Consider the above quote from the *Shâhnâma* where "separation" of one social group from another links only to the priests—they are separated from all other classes (it seems that even today the Iranian Ayatollahs represent this obnoxious 'Aryan' tradition)—and also considering that the Iranian peasants were considered "independent tillers of the soil" just as weavers were said to be "free men" who "labour upon the soil safe from dispute and contest", along with the artisans who are depicted as "given much to thought" (unlike the Indian caste system that is based on the most de-humanized division of labour between physical labour that was said to be unclean;

and mental labour which was said to be of a higher level and thus which was monopolized by the Brahman caste). Clearly the differences between the Iranian and the Indian models are apparent.

The problem is that due to the neurotic structure of caste—one abolishes it only to make it reappear once again—caste makes its presence firstly in liberal India under Nehru and then once again in neo-liberal India in the era of globalization. One thus needs to say that it is not merely the Hindu right-wing led by the RSS and their fascist cousins like the Shiv Sena and the Maharashtra Navnirman Sena that emphasizes caste, but also Gandhi in his silent way who swept it below the carpet of semi-feudal reason, not to forget Nehru who romanticized it as a "system based on services and functions....an all-inclusive order without any common dogma and allowing the fullest latitude to each group". Nehru's romanticism goes on: caste allowed "equality and a measure of freedom; each caste was occupational and applied itself to its own particular work.....(leading) to a high degree of specialization and skill in handicrafts and craftsmanship."[87]

The 'skill' and 'craftsmanship' is not so much of the Indian working classes, but of the Brahmans. If one form of this skilled thinkers and speakers that seem to jump from the 10th mandala of the *Rg Veda* are the skilled Indian liberals, there is also another form that exists in India in the form of the established left. The Brahmans then lie not only with the fascists and the liberals, but also with the established left. In this case the question that Lenin had once raised—*What is to be Done?*—echoes once again.

'Hinduism' as the "Hysterical Sublime"

We need a certain kind of fury that envelops many movements for social and political emancipation. The fury is directed to the exploiters, the counterrevolutionaries, the communal-fascists and imperialist cartels. But the fury is also directed towards the hidden ideologists and the wielders of the ideology of dominance, an ideology of dominance that has led not only to a type of ideological blindness, but also to a silent counter-revolution in India. This silent counterrevolution has been blind to the question of caste and then constructed an imaginary theme of India being a Hindu society. Our claim is that this silent counterrevolution links what Marx once called "idyllic village communities, (that have been the)... the solid foundation of Oriental Despotism, restrain(ing) the human mind within the smallest compass, making it the unresisting tool of superstition, enslaving it beneath traditional rules, depriving it of all grandeur and historical energies"[88] to the imperialist policies of Washington-based think tanks.

What we claim is that in the complete overhauling of the entire ideological superstructure of capitalism, the complete overhauling of the caste system and the ideological myth of Hinduism is absolutely necessary. It is not merely that we argue against imperialism, as if imperialism exists independent of pre-capitalist social formations. One needs to link organically the relation between global capital accumulation, the Indian elites and the ideology of dominance in India. The organic linking of the relation between the economic base of accumulation of capital and the superstructure of the mass hysteria (of "we are Hindus being swamped by Pakistanis and Bangladeshis in our own homeland") and the corresponding stratification, superstition and backwardness needs to be studied.

One needs to link the Yankee War Industry and the Indian ideology in dominance. One thus needs to claim that even the so-called holy book of 'Hinduism' which now the RSS wants to promote as the national book is not in any way to be confused with any sort of philosophical or ethical treatise. One needs to deny the moral claims of the *Gita* as it does nothing but represent the ideological upholding of the caste system. One needs to stress alongside Marx that the caste system "restrains the human mind within the smallest compass". One needs also to emphasize alongside Ambedkar that the claim that the *Gita* is devoid of any message is absolutely correct.[89] It is a "justification of war" and "a philosophical defence of war and killing in war".[90] It is consequently the classical book for the Indian counterrevolution.[91]

To strike at the Ideological State Apparatus (held domestically by both the liberals and the communal-fascists and globally by the American led corporate imperialism) one needs to articulate how this Ideological State Apparatus produces not only this "hysterical melancholia" that we just referred to, but now the construction of what we call after Fredric Jameson as the "hysterical sublime".[92] The production of the discourse of 'Hinduism' (again re-packaged in the early 1990s) as the production of communal identities and the ideology veiling caste and re-packaging graded inequality in this age of late imperialism in permanent crises creates this hysterical sublime. The hysterical sublime crushes all desire for revolution.

So what is this hysterical sublime? It is on the one hand "the experience bordering on terror, the fitful glimpse, in astonishment, stupor and awe of what was so enormous as to crush life altogether."[93] It is also "the limit of figuration and the incapacity of the human mind to give representation."[94] But basically it is a "phantasmatic relationship with some organic pre-capitalist peasant landscape and village society."[95] In this phantasmatic representation, the mass hysteria of "being Hindu" implies a phantasy created by some sort of castration anxiety which is projected elsewhere (i.e. the production of the 'Hindu' as the one who is crushed by the 'Muslim'). This mass hysteria is also the master signifier of the Indian culture industry where people who are unhappy in the unhappy home of capitalism are served with this sense of false happiness. This hysterical sublime is thus what once Marx called *the feeling of ease and strength in human self-estrangement*.[96] One is thus forced to say with cynicism and irony: caste has never left us. Like Freud's eternal recurrence of the neurotic, caste returns to haunt us once again. If Pepsi Cola plays the role of de-politicization in the imperialist bloc of nations, and if the Taliban plays the same role in our neighborhood, it is caste (along with Pepsi Cola and the Indian Taliban) that is playing this role in India.

The Uncanny 'Return' of Leninism

One will have to be really very frank. If one did pay a debt to Fukuyama and the Indian state for re-instating Marxism in a very uncanny way, one needs to pay a form of debt to Žižek and Lars Lih who bring in the figure of Lenin albeit very straight forwardly. But when one brings in Lenin, he is never alone. Besides him are perpetually the figures of Trotsky, Plekhanov, Martov, Luxemburg, Bukharin, et al. And since we are attempting to repeat Lenin (this is Žižek's phrase) without repeating the tragicomic character of neurotic history, one should always have an eraser to remove the figure of Stalin.

One is here trying to conceptualize revolutionary politics, in fact a type of revolutionary politics that goes by the name of Leninist politics, a form of radical politics that despite the criticisms of those who tried to bifurcate the politics of Leninism from the discourses of factory councils and the Soviets goes directly into the domain of a politics of direct action. To try to conceptualize this form of radical politics would also imply that one faces the critiques brought out not only by the western liberal opponents of Leninism, but also those from within the left, from Karl Kautsky and Georgi Plekhanov (for whom the Bolshevik Revolution was premature) to Anton Pannekoek, the Dutch left and G.T. Miasnikov culminating in the alleged followers of Gramsci and the subaltern school.[97] That Antonio Negri and his school of the autonomists in a·way sum up the position of anti-Leninism and in more than one way sum up the issue of anti-Leninism has to be noted.[98]

So what is this Leninism that we are trying to articulate if not to resurrect today in the era of neo-liberal imperialism and the age of post-politics? What is this Leninism that is able to distinguish itself from the Stalinist counterrevolution? To answer this we need to go to the main domain that Althusser reminded us about, the domain that Marx literally discovered—the continent of history. Now those who have read Althusser would know that according to Althusser, Marx follows the two prior discoveries, that of mathematics (discovered by the Greeks) and physics (discovered by Galileo). It is this domain that we turn to, however turning with a slight bourgeois twist.

Now we saw that it was Francis Fukuyama who said that with the downfall of the Soviet experiment and the so-called 'triumph' of neo-liberal capitalism, history it seems had ended. Fukuyama is here both right and wrong, right because the further history of capitalism has most certainly ended (there could be no further room for it to manoeuvre). Marx, as mentioned before, called it the end of the "pre-history" of humanity.[99]

But there is another twist to this tale concocted by Fukuyama. For if he thought that one had to 'return' back to the era of liberalism, then one had with this very same logic of absolute necessity have to face the figures of Lenin, Trotsky, Rosa Luxemburg and the entire repertoire of Revolutionary Marxism. So if the bourgeoisie brought in the figures of liberalism they also brought in the entire repertoire of Revolutionary Marxism. The liberals were then trapped in the very discourse that they themselves thought that they had constructed. Yet one must note that this 'return' of Leninism is not a stale return that comrades from the established left thought, a Leninism that would once again talk of the party of professional revolutionaries and how the workers left to themselves could never reach the stage of revolutionary consciousness (they are doomed to the level of mere trade unionism) and that it was the de-classed bourgeois intellectuals who would bring in communist consciousness from the outside.

The Leninism that we talk of is not this Kautsky-Stalinist rendering. Instead we are talking of a different form of Leninism, in fact a form of *ironical Leninism*, an ironic Leninism that firstly notes Lenin's important aphorism that without understanding the whole of Hegelian dialectics one could never understand Marx, and secondly one bases this Leninism on the body-politics that Marx outlined in his *Economic and Philosophic Manuscripts of 1844*. What is ironic in both these aspects is that Lenin had not read the entire Hegel's *Science of Logic* when he was penning his *What is to be Done?*, nor had he ever come across Marx's *Economic and Philosophic Manuscripts of 1844*. So then how does one construct this form of Leninism, albeit an ironic Leninism? It firstly recognizes the following:

> Certainly none of the major Marxist thinkers of the twentieth century who were also leaders of the parties—not only Leon Trotsky, Luxemburg, Karl Kautsky, or Mao Zedong—with the sole exception of Gramsci (and even then those writings were locked away in prison or in party archives for many years afterwards),

> had made that "return" to the Hegelian dialectic that Marx called "the source of all dialectic." Nor did any of the younger layer of Bolshevik theoreticians, such as Bukharin or Yevgeny Preobrazhensky, make such a move.[100]

Let us "bracket" this return of the ironic Lenin in the 21st century. Let us visit what our actual philosophical basis of the return of Leninism would imply. This thesis would be based on a number of points (some being raised by Žižek):

1. The thesis of the Revolution with a Revolution.
2. History or Historical Materialism to be thought of as a Revolution with a Revolution.
3. Evolutionism is a secularized form of theology.
4. Parliamentary democracy to be understood as a concrete form of evolutionism in the domain of politics.
5. To think of a Marxist philosophy (the "theory" that Lenin talked of in *What is to be Done?*) where Marxist science valorizes itself into a form of dramaturgy.
6. Lenin's thesis of understanding insurrection as an art form.

Communist Philosophy and Lenin's Laughter

To argue for a radical re-politicization of the world by the New Militants, the concept of the proletariat of classical Marxism would have to take broader shape, whereas the multitude the proletariat would encompass Lenin's "all the classes".[101] For one thing, to produce a form of communist militancy one would have to be materialistic and cease being 'ideological'. As we all very well know, Marxist philosophy is not 'ideological'. One does not stick blindly to the idea of class independent of concrete analysis. Consider this classical definition:

> Ideology is a process accomplished by the so-called thinker consciously, it is true, but with a false consciousness. The real motive forces impelling him remain unknown to him: otherwise it simply would not be an ideological process. Here he imagines false or seeming motive forces. Because it is a process of thought he derives its form as well as content from pure thought, either his own or his predecessors. He works with mere thought material, which he accepts without examination as the product of thought,

> and he does not investigate further for a more remote source independent of thought; indeed it is a matter of course to him, because all action is *mediated* by thought, it appears to him to be ultimately based on thought.[102]

To be able to articulate the transcendence of this terrain of the "mere ideological", of "ideology as such" and the problematic of "mere thought"—we could provisionally call it: "surplus thought"—we turn to Lenin in Capri in 1908 three years after the defeated 1905 revolution. The revolution is defeated, repression is at its height and the ultra-left section of the Bolsheviks—Lunacharsky and his comrades—begin to think that "matter has disappeared". They call themselves the "God-seekers". Though they are philosophically conservative, politically they are almost anarchist—they want to abstain from politics. Gorky is also influenced by this god-seeking, politically abstaining philosophy. He meets Lenin and asks him for a "philosophical offer". He wants Lenin to discuss with the 'disappearing anti-materialists'. Lenin's answer? He laughs. We call this Lenin's philosophical laughter. Lenin does not want to talk of philosophy. He thinks that philosophical discussions would weaken the Bolsheviks. But Lenin does write a small tome on philosophy where he defines philosophy as a *Holzweg* or simply a false path. Not only does Lenin want to claim that philosophy is a false path, it is the "falsest of false paths" (*Holzweg der Holzwege*) and the "professors of philosophy" are "graduated flunkeys" who "stultify people by their torturous 'idealism'."[103] Philosophers are not only graduated flunkeys, but also torturers. They torture with their idealisms. They become like Shakespeare's Cassius where the philosophers as graduate flunkeys appear as Cassius with a "lean and hungry look" who "thinks too much", forgetting that "such men can be dangerous".[104] Lenin refuses to engage in ideological games of creating "surplus thought".

So what does Lenin propose to do? He of course does not want to think too much. Instead, he proposes a different practice of philosophy. Now we know that Althusser has narrated us this little bit on both Lenin and the different practice of philosophy. But Althusser himself being an academic philosopher cannot conceive what this different practice is. He cannot understand dialectical materialism and Marx's tremendous scientific revolution because he himself remains an academic. He does not understand the relation between science and aesthetics. He can most certainly talk of the revolution, but he cannot talk of the Revolution with a Revolution. He thus cannot link philosophy—especially the different practice of philosophy—with class struggle. He remains an ideologist. He cannot understand what radical philosophy is, what the Leninist party is, what the most modern science is.

It is from this conjuncture that we turn to the construction of a radical philosophy that grasps the masses by the roots. In this sense we turn from philosophy as torturous idealism to radical praxis. For this we need to understand what the young Marx had once said. According to Marx, a radical break is necessary in human understanding. One had to have a complete upheaval. So to understand philosophy one had to learn the art of literally transcending philosophy by realizing it. Now what does this mean? It means that one learns praxis, to be precise revolutionary praxis.

But then what is the relation between philosophy—to be precise Marxist philosophy, or the theory that Lenin talked of without which there could be no revolution—and revolutionary praxis? To understand this one needs to go into Marx's celebrated revolution in philosophy and the formation that he had outlined in his *A Contribution to the Critique of Hegel's Philosophy of Right. Introduction.* Before we understand the two terms in German (in this text) that form the basics of revolutionary dialectics, it is important that one needs to understand what is called the "most radical rupture with traditional ideas".[105] It is this grand paradigm shift, this "terrain shift" that Althusser loved calling, whereby one understands both the different practice of philosophy as well the possibilities of revolutionary praxis.

Let us have a look at these two terms: (1) *Aufhebung* that is translated as "sublation-transcendence-supersession", and (2) *Verwirklichung* which implies simply an "actualization" or "realization". The first one is what Hegel had introduced in his

Science of Logic where he talked of *Aufhebung* as an essential process embedded in history (in fact which forms the basics of the motor force of history). Now according to this dialectical logic of *Aufhebung* reality is "lifted up" at a higher level of existence through the double process of cancellation and preservation. Both Marxist philosophy and revolutionary praxis "lifts up" reality at a higher level, the level from capitalism and the dehumanization of the production of commodities to the site of world revolution.

Now every Marxist should understand this dialectics of history in order to situate oneself in a proper historical context. What I have called the politics of revolutionary desire—or simply desireology—is constituted in this dialectics of history. And that is why I have slightly modified the philosophy and science of dialectical and historical materialism as *dialectical and historical-humanist materialism.* In more than one way I relate this with Gramsci's historicism and humanism and Raya Dunayevskaya's Marxist-Humanism. In the most prominent way Marxism then is understood as the critique of mechanical materialism and the theory of the "iron laws" of history. One develops a philosophy of praxis. The Communist Party, to be precise the Marxist Leninist Party becomes the party of action. It transforms the Enlightenment theme of the "'man' of action" into the theory of the *party of action*. Our theme will now flow to this site of the party of action which understands the role of the party as what Karl Korsch once called, "*human sensuous activity, as praxis*".[106]

It is here that one is able to differentiate the revolutionary Leninist party from the parties of revisionism and parliamentary democracy. In contrast to these revisionists who more than dealing with dynamic social reality, deal with the realm of the 'ideological' (and the fixation with 'ideas'), Revolutionary Marxism teaches us the materialization and humanization of 'ideas'. It does not talk of the 'ideas' of god, the soul, the nature of reality, etc. Instead it talks of what the good society should be all about and then says that communism is this good society. And because Marxism is always people-friendly and because it puts the hopes and desires of humanity at the centre of its revolutionary politics, it learns to encounter the collective conscious of the working masses as well as the deep unconscious. What we now say is that Marxism should not at all deal with 'consciousness' and 'ideologies'. Instead one goes into the deep desires of the working masses. One then goes to the triple critiques of human alienation (the split of one human from the other), political economy (the study of the accumulation of capital) and the unconscious (what our desires are all about).

To understand this let us deepen the Marxist understanding of ideology as false consciousness. We have this concept now being further realized as the new definition of ideology that emerges in *Capital*: "We are not aware of this, nevertheless we do it". (*Sie wissen das nicht, aber sie tun es*)[107]. Ideology is thus not about being aware, but it is about the repression of this awareness. If on the one hand we are dealing with the politics of the unconscious, we have now with the triumph of the Global Media Industry a new definition of ideology: "They know it, yet they do it!"[108] Now the Marxist revolutionary will have to understand that it is both these contexts that have to be dealt with. We have to deal with the unconscious (the first definition from Marx: ideology is unawareness, the realm of the unconscious) as well as with a type of what we know after Žižek as an "enlightened false consciousness" or simply a petty bourgeois cynicism.

And that is also why we say, as we had earlier said, that one understands the unconscious and then moves from the politics of the unconscious to the revolutionary site of desire.[109] And that is also why we say that Revolutionary Marxism is all about revolutionary desire. When Lenin insisted in *What is to be Done?* on the role of the professional revolutionary he implied the art of desiring, that leads to the aesthetics of insurrection. In this sense one would disagree with Rosa Luxemburg here who reduces Lenin's theory of party to a form of what she calls "military ultra-centralism"[110] One will also disagree with Luxemburg's opposition of "centralism" to "autonomist tendencies".[111]

The Leninist party is not an abstraction, an *Absolute and Abstract Universal* independent of individuals and classes. Instead one has to understand the Leninist party as the *Concrete*

Universal which combines the individual (real people) with the particular (the concrete conjuncture of classes) and the general (history and humanity).[112] The party is no mediator, Hegelian or otherwise.[113] In this very dialectical way the party also takes the humanist form of species being where people are related to one another way as people, and not in the capitalist form of a reified and distorted form, a relation between things (money, class, caste, gender domination, political power, etc.).

Here this philosophical Leninism relates to the classical philosophical questions of the true, the good and the beautiful, determined by the question: "how is free humanity possible?"; and with the character of the New Social System called Communism. The Leninist party is not a bureaucratic ultra-centralist organization, but the organization where the dialectical centre sublates (*aufheben*) itself in the whole of society, where the party becomes the masses and the masses become the party. The party is thus understood as the mode of appearance of the insurrectionist masses. The art of insurrection remains at the basis of this historicist and humanist logic.

This art is primarily a solution to bourgeois cynicism and to the spectacle of late imperialism in permanent crisis. One is not dealing anymore with 'consciousness', the consciousness whether Narendra Modi is good or not good. One is now in the midst of desire. Thus one is not interested any more in changing 'consciousness'. The left ideologist who intends to 'teach' the worker about his/her own situation is nothing but the bourgeois educator who remains perpetually bourgeois. In this sense we not only transcend the mechanical types of politics that was evident in Bukharin, but we also transcend the problem of the reification of consciousness that Lukács had made central to his *History and Class Consciousness*.

The Problem of Parliamentary Democracy

What needs to be done is to link the question of traditional philosophy that Lenin laughed at, this traditional thinking that remains at the basis of Hamlet's existentialist dilemma with the psychoanalytic questions of paranoia and neurosis. Since Hamlet is an idealist—plagued by the ghost of his father—he cannot conceive of radical praxis. The art of insurrection is totally foreign to him. He cannot understand that:

> Democracy is a contradiction in itself, an untruth, nothing but hypocrisy at the bottom. Political liberty is sham liberty, the worst form of slavery. The contradiction must come out in the form of real equality in the form of communism.[114]

What traditional thinking (like parliamentary democracy) does is that it does not understand the deep structure of class societies. It does not bother to understand the difference between the abstract and the concrete. It therefore does not bother to know what this political liberty is and how as abstract reality it is governed by the contradiction between capital and labour. What traditional thinking does is that it is seized by what Marx calls "independent beings (*selbständige Gestalten*) endowed with life."[115] The traditional thinker imagines that this political liberty is a reality, and when he finds out that this form of political liberty in the age of neo-liberal capitalism takes violent forms (often realized as the politics of communal-fascism), he is terrorized by these very strange beings. He becomes what Jean Hyppolite once called a "mentally estranged person", caught in the "enchanted topsy-turvy world" where Monsieur Capital and Madame Rent are found doing their "ghost-walking" all over the globe.[116] Hamlet seeks to flee, but is chained not only to the capital flows of the phantom commodity, but also chained to the psychotic flows that capitalism necessarily creates. He is reified, not as an insect as in Kafka's *Metamorphosis*, but as some sort of modern 'man' who lives in "the world of illusions, half-truths and unsolved contradictions feeling completely at home in these estranged and irrational forms"[117]. This 'modern man' then evolves into a primitive 'cave man'. He rushes into the cave dwelling of liberalism, namely the parliament, "a dwelling which remains an alien power", "a dwelling which he cannot regard as his own hearth":

> We have said that humanity (like Hamlet—the traditional philosopher and parliamentarian par excellence, my insertion, M.J.) is regressing into the *cave dwelling*, etc.—but he is regressing to it in an estranged, malignant form. The savage in his cave—a natural element which freely offers itself for his use and

> protection—feels himself no more a stranger, or rather feels as much at home as a *fish in water*. But the cellar dwelling of the poor man is a hostile element, "a dwelling which remains an alien power and only gives itself up to him insofar as he gives his blood and sweat"—a dwelling which he cannot regard as his own hearth—where he might at last exclaim: "Here I am at home"—but where instead finds in *someone else's* home, in the house of a *stranger* who always watches him and throws him out if he does not pay his rent.[118]

To understand this very strange and paranoid scene let us turn back to Marx's idea of the fetishism of commodities where products of the imagination have been reified as monstrous beings endowed with life of their own. Let us then relate this with Freud on the mentally ill person, especially his theory of the "neuropsychoses of defence" where paranoia is understood as a "neurosis of defence" whose chief mechanism is projection. What we Marxist Leninists do is link this neurosis-paranoia with the commodity form and the logic of the accumulation of capital. In this sense we translate Marx's classical historical materialist statement: *the economic base determines the political and ideological superstructure* into the new Freudo-Marxist statement: *the reified base of capital accumulation determines the paranoid mind of the parliamentary counterrevolutionary.*

There are two sites that determine the makings of this paranoid mind:

1. Fetishized perception where Hamlet as the exemplary estranged person perceives the 'eternally' recurring signifier (M^1) in the circuit of capital: $M\text{-}C\text{-}M^1$. Now we know from the very first pages of *Capital* that this M^1 'eternally' recurs as M^2, M^3, M^4....etc., and that this 'eternally' recurring $M^{1\,2\,3\,4}$.....; is both a monstrous thing that loses its bodily form, and in this psychotic form of complete alienation and disembodiment, becomes a ghost.[119] Now it is important to note that this fetishized occulting process of the neurotic-psychotic recurrence of capital takes an "independent" (*Selbständige*) form, an independence that is totally alienated from real people. And it is this fetishized occultation process that the

Leninist New Militants grasp as the chaotic (wrongly stated as "anarchic" or "spontaneous") world of bourgeoisdom. It transforms this chaos into the spontaneous activity of the masses and the communist labour of the negative. But Hamlet just simply refuses to engage Lenin and is seized by the paranoia and fear of insurrectionist power regresses as the neurotic and psychotic taking refuge in the parliament.

2. This is the second site that we recognize—the site of the *Reified-Psychotic Unconscious*. Here estranged humanity *projects* onto the superstructural parliamentary world what is actually *denied* in the bourgeois world. So what is denied in the real world (the entire regime of rights: equality, liberty and fraternity) is projected in the duplicated and distorted world of the parliament. This parliamentary superstructure is also understood as a *symbolic-investiture*, invested with magical and fetishized powers. Thus the more people are denied economic and political rights; the more is projected onto this estranged parliamentary life-world. What we have now is this *lack (denial)/power* bi-polarity where the lack exists in the real economic base and this fetishized 'imagined' power in the political superstructure. That is why Lenin continuously talked of "parliamentary cretinism". He tells the world revisionists, the Bernsteins and Kautskys, that this 'imagined' parliament can never give them socialist power.

The world revisionists, the Bernsteins and Kautskys, produce this *Denkfaul* ("mental laziness") that refuses to transcend the site of reification. Now those versed with Freudo-Marxism will know that there is a similarity between Marx's critique of reified consciousness and Freud's idea of mental illness. In *The Uncanny (das Unheimlich)*, Freud talks of the mental patient who fantasizes that life has been given to lifeless objects. He feels that some object, that in reality is only an object, has truly life of its own. Here Freud's patient is filled with the feeling of dread.

Let us go to Freud in order that we understand why the parliamentary leftist fears the Revolution with a Revolution.

Freud calls this the "uncanny". The uncanny according to Freud is "related to what is frightening—to what arouses dread and horror... It tends to coincide with what excites fear in general"[120]. There is an "unknown nature of the uncanny"[121]. Further the uncanny is "that class of the frightening which leads us back to what is known of old and long familiar"[122]. Freud explains the term "uncanny" in various languages. In Greek it implies the "strange" and "foreign", in English it means "uncomfortable", "uneasy", "gloomy", "dismal", "ghostly", "haunted", while in Arabic and Hebrew the uncanny means the same as "daemonic" and "gruesome"[123]. In opposition to this strange world of the dead which is given life is *Heimlich*. It indicates that which "belongs to the house", "not strange", "familiar", "tame", "intimate", "friendly", "well", "free from fear", "familiar", "amicable", etc.[124] In *Unheimlich* the negative character is held: "eerie", "weird", "arousing gruesome fear", "ghostly", "motionless like a stone image", "secret and hidden", etc. Freud quotes Schelling, " *"Unheimlich" is the name of everything that ought to have remained...secret and hidden but has come to light"*.[125]

The main theme linking Freud's analysis of the uncanny with Marx's estranged mind is found in Freud's statement, whether "an apparently animate being is really alive; or conversely, whether a lifeless object might not be in fact animate".[126] And what happens in this realm of the lifeless object that appears endowed with life? The person becomes mentally estranged and is seized by the "phantom of horror".[127] And it is here that we understand the politics of the parliamentary leftists. This horror of being estranged is also the horror of the complete loss of the self. In this realm of the loss, a process of doubling and duplication takes place. Consider how Marx's "cave", the "non-home" which becomes the "home", becomes the parliament where one has sought refuge. We knew that earlier, religion was the place where one sought refuge, now the parliament has become the religion in the age of late imperialism in permanent crisis.

Let us see Marx's dialectic at work. In Marx: there is the process of self-alienation (*Selbstentfremdung*), whereby one has the "duplication (*Verdoppelung*) of the world" into an "imaginary world" and a "real (*weltliche*) one".[128] We thus have two worlds: (1) the real one: the world of the workplace, the slums, the retrenchment of workers, etc., and (2) the imaginary one: the world of the parliament. What we get is a "self-cleavage" (*Selbstzerrissenheit*) and "self-contradictoriness" (*Sichselbstwidersprechen*) in the heart of our Hamlet, the Prince of Revisionism. In this self-cleavage, the class structure of society detaches (*abhebt*) itself and establishes itself in the clouds as an "independent realm" (*selbständiges Reich*)[129] as the temple of parliamentary democracy. Hamlet takes the form of the *Doppelcharakter*[130], this lying schizophrenic double character, this double character, who loses all sense of concrete reality, loses his real body and gets plagued by his imaginary-deluded mind.

A Small Note on Marx's Critique of Idealist and Speculative Philosophy

One now needs to consider Marx's critique of reification in general, and then relate this theme of Hamlet-Freud with Marx's critique of speculative philosophy itself. From this we understand how the schizoid split takes place in society bifurcating the economic base from the ideological superstructure, thus getting the logic of self-alienation that creates the two worlds: the imagined-deluded world and the real world:

> Two souls alas, are housed within my breast,
> And each will wrestle for the mastery there.[131]

But wait! Have we not seen the similar type of critique of philosophy engaged by Marx? Did not Marx in the *Contribution to the Critique of Hegel's Doctrine of the State* critique Hegel for involving the process of inverted thinking? Did Marx not say that Hegel involves a mystification? And is this mystification nothing but an inversion? Does one not relate the mystification and inversion of philosophical thinking expressed as the estranged mind, with the inversion of bourgeois reality itself? Consider Marx, in Hegel the following pairs are inverted: subject/object, being/consciousness, empirical/transcendent, material/ideal, finite/infinite, existence/essence, determinate/

determined, etc., to get the reversed pairs: object/subject, consciousness/being, transcendent/empirical, etc., etc. Now not only is there an inversion, but also an erasure within each of the pairs to posit the world in the "form of the object". What is left is the *transcendent-idealized-essence*. The world appears as the hypostatized estranged signifier. So when Marx says that for Hegel reality appears as "the Idea", claiming to be an "independent subject", and functioning as the "demiurgos of the real world (*der Demiurg des Wirklichen*)", he is saying that Hegel's importance is found in the epistemological process of the mystification-inversion, which is a mere superstructure for a deeper structural inversion. And this inversion implies a "personification of the thing and the reification (*Verdinglichung*) of the person".[132]

What we get is this: mystification=inversion=reification= depersonification of the human and the personification of the thing. And for Marx, like Freud, the estranged and reified object would turn out to be the source of the distortion and reification of consciousness. In this way Marx draws the importance of the reading of philosophy (as the estranged and deluded mind) so as to look into the estrangement of reality itself. The philosopher as the 'philosopher's philosopher' is now not the disinterested philosopher seeking the philosopher's stone but the ideologist. The philosopher constructs the logic of the reified mind. The ideologist creates the mass consciousness of bourgeois society. In this way the philosopher, both as the 'philosopher's philosopher' as well as the ideologist becomes the embodiment and spokesperson of this distortion and bourgeoisiefication.

Faust as the New Messiah

If however the parliamentary leftist has become totally useless to the radical democratic movement, if the parliamentary leftist is seized by what Max Horkheimer called a "mimetic impulse"[133] to the Hamletean tragedy; then in comes Faust as the revolutionary terrorist who has total disdain for Hamlet's estranged character. The parliamentarian leftist is bewildered by the ghost of the welfare state that he sees everywhere and is frightened by Claudius, the neo-liberal state who is carrying out havoc, here, in the land of Gandhi. If Marcellus could say that "something is rotten in the state of Denmark"[134], then the parliamentarian leftist says that "something is rotten in the neo-liberal state". This modern-day Hamlet then screams: "My father's spirit in arms! All is not well".[135] He hears the voice of the ghost of the welfare-state:

> I am thy father's spirit;
> Doom'd for a certain term to walk the night,
> And for the day confin'd to fast in fires,
> Till the foul crimes done in my days of nature
> Are burnt and purg'd away. But that I am
> forbid
> To tell the secrets of my prison-house.[136]

The parliamentarian wants to hear the secrets of the death of welfare capitalism. But the once-upon-a-time friend and comrade of Hamlet, namely, Faust the revolutionary terrorist, knows all the secrets. The revolutionary terrorist is not only like Faust, he is also like Sergey Nechaev who has imbibed Dostoevsky's characterization of Raskolnikov from *Crime and Punishment*. He wants rivers of blood to flow.[137] He fantasizes that power flows from the barrel of a gun. He wants to understand "contradictions" and the true nature of "practice". But being inspired by Raskolnikov (whose name means the "divided self") he once again indulges in pure fantasy and imagines that a 'radical' act is performed by killing an old woman. He is not only what Walter Benjamin called the "master of his powers", but also "man enough to blast open the continuum of history".[138] This is what the revolutionary terrorist does:

> Who would have believed it! We are told that new Joshuas
> at the foot of every tower, as though irritated with
> time itself, fired at the dials in order to stop the day.[139]

The revolutionary terrorist wants to annihilate class enemies. The whole method is secretive and conspiratorial. As Charu Mazumdar, the founder of this New Joshua movement in India, had once said: "He who has not dipped his hands in the blood of class enemies can hardly be called a communist".[140] Like Faust the figure of the devil does not frighten him:

> And shall I, thing of flame, flinch at the sequel?
> My name is Faust, in everything your equal.[141]

The philosophy of the 'deed' is central to this Faustian theme:

> 'Tis writ, 'In the beginning was the Word.'
> I pause, to wonder what is here inferred.
> The word I cannot set supremely high:
> A new translation I will try.
> I read, if by the spirit I was taught,
> This opening I need to weigh again,
> Or sense may suffer from a hasty pen.
> Does thought create, and work, and rule the hour?
> 'Twere best: 'In the beginning was the power.'
> Yet while the pen is urged with willing fingers,
> A sense of doubt and hesitancy lingers.
> The spirit comes to guide me in my need,
> I write, 'In the beginning was the deed'.[142]

And yet though Faust has become 'radical', in the sense that he has gone beyond the 'word' directly to the 'deed', his 'deed' is an *estranged deed*. He acts as Marx once said like the commodity-owners: "They therefore acted and transacted before they thought".[143] So what does this very radical but estranged person do? He involves in conspiracies. Consider Marx:

> The chief characteristic of the conspirators' way of life is their battle with the police, to whom they have precisely the same relationship as thieves and prostitutes. The police tolerate the conspiracies, and not just as a necessary evil: they tolerate them as centers which they can keep under easy observation and where the most violent revolutionary elements in society meet, as the forges of revolt, which in France has become a tool of government quite as the police themselves, and finally as a recruiting place for their own political informers....... The conspirators are constantly in touch with the police, they come into conflict with them all the time; they hunt the informers, just as the informers hunt them. Spying is one of their main occupations. It is no wonder therefore that the short step from being a conspirator by trade to being a paid police spy is so frequently made facilitated as it is by poverty and prison, by threats and promises.[144]

While this conspirator plans to conquer the fear of death, he appears not merely as a poet-thief, but as the one who claims to "blast a specific life out of the era".[145] This Faustian-figure "recognizes the sign of the Messianic cessation of happening".[146] He loathes Hamlet's paranoia and neurosis. He is the creator of "Messianic time".[147] Since the Indian state understands that this messiah is not part of the fascist genre, this very liberal and tolerant state declares Faust a menace to be destroyed. But Faust wants to be destroyed. The destroyer and the destroyed need one another. After all capitalism wants spectacles to exist. And both the 'destroyer' and the 'destroyed' (the great contradiction from this tragi-farce) will enact this great spectacle. What one has to understand is that just as neo-liberalism needs Faustian characters, just as it needs the modern-day popes and czars, French radicals and German police spies; Faust too needs the devil.

Faust strikes at not only the continuum of history, but strikes at history too. He also strikes at the devil. But it is actually a deal which he has struck. The cunning of history has returned once again. Faust (now very strangely due to his hyper-imagination) metamorphosizes into Hamlet and "waxes desperate with imagination".[148] The Indian state also loves hyper-imagination. It also loves these "alchemists of the revolution". It cries out that the alchemists are going to toss bombs. It produces nursery tales that Faust is a Red Specter.

Leninism and Marx's Dramaturgy

And since the Indian state has cried out that the revolution has come to strike out all that is holy and good, one needs to recall Marx's celebrated: "A specter is haunting Europe, the specter of Communism. All the Powers of old Europe have entered into a holy alliance to exorcize this specter: Pope and czar, Metternich and Guizot, French Radicals and German police-spies."[149] And it is this Red Specter that has woken the Indian state from its very liberal slumber that suddenly made the Indian state to deal with what they think is a menace. The state calls the modern popes and czars, French radical thinkers and German fascism to deal with this terrible menace.

According to Marx and Engels: "Two things result from this fact:

I. Communism is already acknowledged by all European Powers to be itself a Power.
II. It is high time that Communists should openly, in the face of the whole world, publish their views, their aims, their tendencies, and meet this nursery tale of the specter of Communism with a Manifesto of the party itself."[150]

What one does is that one produces a form of revolutionary desire in this act of considering itself a Revolutionary Power. One moves from the politics of the unconscious to the revolutionary site of desire. It is here that we transform the hitherto known Lenin (the so-called Jacobin Lenin who then changed his views of the party). We understand Leninism as revolutionary desire. That is why we are saying that when he insisted in *What is to be Done?* on the role of the professional revolutionary he implied the art of desiring. This art is primarily a solution to bourgeois cynicism and to the spectacle of late imperialism in permanent crisis. One is not dealing any more with 'consciousness'. One is now in the midst of desire. Thus one is not interested any more in changing 'consciousness'. The left ideologist who intends to 'teach' the worker about his own situation is nothing but the bourgeois educator who remains perpetually bourgeois.

So instead of ideas and ideologies one puts "the real, corporeal *human being*" with its "real objective *essential powers*" (*wirklichen gegenstandlichen Wesenkräfte*)[151] at the centre of revolutionary politics. Marx's will to revolutionary power now enters the scene of revolution. Instead of ideologies we have the *natural powers* (*naturlichen Kräften*) and *vital powers* (*Lebenskräften*)"[152], or simply "human essential powers" (*menschlichen Wesenkrafte*) [153] of the proletariat on this new scene of revolution. The theme of consciousness is now transcended for a theory of human essential powers.

And since the "ontological essence of human passion (*Leidenschaft*) coming into being"[154] is now our focus, we say that the revolutionary party is also the party of passion. As passion it immediately confronts both capital accumulation and the state. In contrast to hitherto existing left discourse—whether Stalin, Trotsky or Mao inspired—our theme of the immediate abolishing of the state remains central to our reading of Leninism. For it is the state (as the organizing committee of the passionless bourgeoisie) that thwarts the passions of the revolution.

Before we construct this form of Marxist dramaturgy one will have a have a small note on this Leninism. Leninism is this Real of the Revolution (a Real that has within it both the body and the mind—one cannot have a Cartesian dualism here—or the authentic self of this real politics) where Marx's use-value of *Capital* is related to the idea of the professional revolutionary that goes beyond the employer/employee relation and goes directly into the domain of the circuit of capital (M-C-M^{1}) and the state. What Lenin did throughout his life is that he thought of this concrete universal: capital/state; i.e. capital as such and state as such. His thesis is not the empiricist one of Kautsky, nor the Kantian one of form (here revolutionary consciousness) coming from the outside and latching onto the social content (the proletariat movement). Let us reflect on this:

> It may sound the same, but it is not: in Kautsky, there is no space for politics proper, just the combination of the social (working class and its struggle, from which intellectuals are implicitly excluded) and the pure neutral classes, subjective knowledge of these intellectuals. In Lenin on the contrary, "intellectuals" are themselves caught in the conflict of ideologies (i.e. the ideological class struggle) which is unsurpassable.[155]

What do we have here? Kautsky cannot grasp the space of "politics proper". Lenin grasps this realm. The Red Specter appears once again. And because the Indian state is preaching absolute and unconditional non-violence and since Communism ceases to be a nursery tale, but a declared Power, one needs to go into the dynamics of Leninist praxis that openly calls for a dictatorship of the proletariat.

In *The Legacy of Karl Marx* I had said that one needs to let a very radical form of Marxism intervene—Marxism Leninism to be precise, where the party of insurrection will realize communism as humanism and naturalism.[156] And because, as we noted earlier, that with messianic capitalism announcing the return of liberalism, the irony of this repeating history postulated a counter perspective to the liberal narrative: not the return of the bankers, popes and czars, but the return of the revolutionaries, thus the return of Leninism and the revolutionary party. And because with the return of Lenin one sees complete bourgeois intolerance against both radical politics and Leninism, one has another form of intolerance: Leninist intolerance, intolerance to global capitalism, and to liberals, neocons and fascists alike. Here I recall Žižek's notion of Leninist intolerance.[157] 'Tolerance' is not about real tolerance, not about real humanity, not about equality of all religions, etc. which the state always preaches and never practices. 'Tolerance' here is about the spectacle of capitalism, about forgetting revolution, forgetting the overproduction of commodities and with it the overproduction of the regression of critical thinking. Leninist intolerance is about this very radical critique of regressive thinking. So when Lenin had said in *What is to be Done?* that one has to seek a very modern science, a Theory (with a capital "T"), he also meant that one had to always combat this regressive thinking. Lenin calls it "the most advanced theory".[158] One does not only have to combat the ideologies of the czars and the popes, not only combat royalty and religion. One has to combat this tolerance for the popes and the czars, of royalty and religion. To be humanist, in the very Marxist sense, one has to be combative, combative of this liberal notion of tolerance. It ponders over the following observation:

> Fidelity to the democratic consensus means the acceptance of the present liberal-parliamentary consensus, which precludes any serious questioning of how this liberal-democratic order is complicit in the phenomena it officially condemns and, of course, any serious attempt to imagine a society whose socio-political order would be different.[159]

It is this very juncture that I articulate historical materialism as a Revolution with a Revolution from a very different perspective than what usually Marxists, post-Lenin, thought. We talk of a New Science of desireology that perfects the art of insurrection and transcends the Old Science of ideology. We claim that the Old Discipline thought, and only thought, thought only of thought—thought in the abstract. They thought of the thought of liberalism, fascism, socialism, etc, but they could never think about socialism. We know that this is the theme that Marx and Engels laid out in *The German Ideology*. The ideologists thought that the whole world is comprised of thoughts and to change the world, one only had to change thoughts. What did the ideologists do? They thought of revolution, a revolution that occurred many times each day in their terribly clever craniums. Their revolution—i.e. the revolution of the ideologists—was a Revolution without a Revolution. We know that Marx and Engels wrote an entire tome of it called *The German Ideology*. We also know that Engels called ideology "false consciousness"[160]. And yet we somehow claim that Marxism is an ideology.

And it is this legacy that Lenin picks up. Marx's idea of human essential powers of the working class that comprehends a mass struggle against capitalism, is realized as the Power that Marx and Engels spelled out in the *Manifesto*. It is then actualized as the party of *direct action*. We use this term "desireology" so as to understand the relation between science and art—especially on the idea of human sensibility of Marx's *Economic and Philosophic Manuscripts of 1844*. If classical aesthetics deals with the beautiful and the culture industry deals with the ridiculous—what the Frankfurt School called "pacifying rebellious desire"—desireology as the art of insurrection deals with what Lenin in *The April Theses* called the *Augenblick* or the unique chance of revolution.[161]

And since the "ontological essence of human passion (*Leidenschaft*) coming into being"[162] is now our focus, we say that the revolutionary party is also the party of sublime passion. The world revolution is the realization of this passion. Passion is of course related to humanity at large, with humanity as humanity. It is this humanity as humanity which Marx called, "the human essence" (*das menschliche Wesen*) and communism as the realization of this human essence. Understanding this humanism of Marx, one claims that the question of the good society is central to Marxism. Of course we know that this understanding has not to be confused with utopian conceptions, for any references to what one may vaguely call 'stupid sentiments' is alien to Marxism. I keep this idea of the good society that is devoid of 'stupid sentiments' as not only central, but also central in a very contradictory way. Recall what Lenin had said to Gorky about the great European composer Beethoven so as to understand this contradiction. Lenin talks of knowing Beethoven's *Appassionata* sonata "inside out", and yet he states that, "he is willing to listen to it every day" because it is "wonderful, ethereal music". Lenin then wonders how people can "produce such marvels!" Yet Lenin involves a rather strange sort of contradiction and then winks and laughs at Gorky saying that he was unable to listen to music, since it got on his nerves. After all, Lenin, the Lenin who practiced the art of insurrection, would like to stroke his "fellow beings and whisper sweet nothings in their ears for being able to produce such beautiful things in spite of the abominable hell they are living in". Yet Lenin warns that "one shouldn't caress anybody—for people will only bite off your hand; strike, without pity, although theoretically we are against any kind of violence. Oh, it is, in fact, an infernally difficult task!"[163]

And it is this "infernally difficult task" of wanting to caress people living in "abominable hell", and yet striking without pity (though theoretically being against violence) that propels us to see what Marx discovered, such that one "strikes without pity" even when you want to "stroke my fellow beings". One must state here that a moral dilemma is noted that there was, as Lukács said, "no hatred in Lenin. He fought against institutions and this, naturally, meant that he also had to fight against the men who represented those institutions—if necessary to their annihilation. But he always considered it a humanly deplorable necessity even though it could not be avoided or disregarded under certain concrete conditions."[164]

How to Transcend History as Tragicomedy

We return to the realm of "desireology"[165]—the realm that grasps the Real of desires—that is contrasted to the old discipline of ideology, a discipline that is idealist through and through, in fact nothing but a form of re-packaged mythology and theology. In contrast "desireology" is nothing but a form of revolutionary materialism and the communism that is both humanism and naturalism that is directly bent towards action.

One therefore has to talk of transcending the old discipline of ideology as also those of liberal democracy, parliamentarism and Stalinism. I shall not here mention Maoism because it creates a form of a "shock" to the good old liberal order that the Indian state seeks to promote. This "shock" may not be a "dialectical shock" (to borrow Fredric Jameson's term from a different context), but a shock nevertheless. It is a shock to the old liberals, for the children of the Indian republic have turned this republic into a wild kindergarten and struck by infantile disorder are shooting and bombing the republic's own 'caretakers'. But what I said was the following:

> The tragicomic idea of history has a very rigorously defined structure—the structure of being haunted by the past of 'old politics'—the structure of the old politics of liberalism, transfigured communism and fascism. One has debates more on the politics of multi-party democracy and its binary: authoritarianism than on mass politics. What happens is a peculiar type of political distortion that does not remain merely on the political plain. It penetrates into every area of the human life-world. This distortion—that Lukács had immortalized as the reification of consciousness and a feeling of helplessness and known since Freud as the feeling of dread and terror, or simply the feeling of the uncanny (*das Unheimlich*)—remains the dominant part of class history even today. One needs to go to the roots of this distortion and the dominance of the uncanny type of tragicomic history and consequently to treat the question of revolution, not as economism and parliamentarism, but as *cultural and aesthetical education determined by the critique of political economy and the historical class struggle*. It recalls Marx's dictum: to produce according to "the laws of beauty". It is then that one understands the Leninist politics of treating insurrection as art. Revolutionary politics becomes a dramaturgy—a theatre of the "Real", where "the sublime feeling of enthusiasm" is able to realize itself.[166]

But how indeed does one transcend the tragicomic structure of history, how does one transcend economism, parliamanterism, all the blah blahs of parliamentary cretinism? How does one openly declare the parliament as what Lenin in *State and Revolution* called "talk shops of political prostitution"?[167] What then is this New Space that Marx discovered that is neither the space of civil society where the Anna Hazares and the Indian Rasputins along with retired generals do their macabre dance, nor is it the state where the cousins of the Rasputins and the retired generals create their talk shops?

To understand the transcendence of this tragicomic character of history one needs to highlight a few terms. But firstly one has to understand Marx's very important question: "Why does humanity appear "upside down" or literally "standing on its head" (*auf den Kopf gestellt erscheinen*)?"[168] Secondly it is about terminology and the rational and human character of Hegelian dialectics. Principally *Aufhebung* implies a "lifting up", in which there is a transcendence, which *preserves* as well as *abolishes* reality at a *higher* level of being. For Hegel, *Aufhebung* "has a twofold meaning....on the one hand it means to preserve, to maintain, and equally it also means to cause to cease, to put an end to. Even "to preserve" includes a negative element, namely, that something is removed from its immediacy and so from an existence which is open to external influences, in order to preserve it".[169]

So in order to transcend this tragicomic character of history, one needs to employ multiple *aufheben*. One follows *On the Jewish Question* where we understand an "*Aufhebung* of religion"[170], and an "*aufzuheben* of these real distinctions"[171], while in *A Contribution to the Critique of Hegel's Philosophy of Right. Introduction* Marx reiterates the "*Aufhebung* of religion as the (abolition) of the illusory happiness of the people".[172] In the *Economic and Philosophic Manuscripts of 1844* we read the "positive *Aufhebung* of all estrangement"[173], followed by the "transcendence of all classes" (*Aufhebung aller Klassen*)[174] along with the explosive "*Aufhebung* of the basis" itself.[175]

And that is why we state that this principle of the complete transcendence of estrangement with the *Aufhebung* of private property (*Aufhebung des Privateigentums*) and the state (*Aufhebung des Staates*)[176] remains the condition and sine qua non of Revolutionary Marxism. Humanity has itself to be understood as perpetual transcendences.[177] And it is this idea of perpetual transcendences and upheavals that Lenin had argued for.

To contextualize the question of the parliament inspired reified mind, to understand how the reification (anti-praxis) of not only consciousness, but the reification of humanity's very being and consequently the reification of political praxis takes place, let us concretely understand the *very physical space* of this reification and how the transcendence of reification can take place. This is the central dialectic in Marx: where there is "the estrangement of the human essence" (*die Entfremdung des menschliche Wesens*)—the shooting-down of workers by gendarmes—and "the transcendence of this estrangement" (*die Aufhebung des Entfremdung*) which is also understood as "the appropriation of the human essence" (*die Aneignung des menschliche Wesens*)[178]. Getting back this human essence is to get it back in terms of a political praxis, the praxis of the Revolution with the Revolution.

Revolutionary dialectics confronts capitalism. It does not wait for the so-called "inevitable" revolutions. It is not cowardly like Stalinism. It utterly disbelieves in the counterrevolutionary thesis of socialism-in-one-country. It is praxis-oriented. Unlike the Stalinists who are contemplative, it deals with active organization for the overthrow of world capitalism. Unlike the Indian left (who in their pretentious opposition to imperialism) it does not support Third World reactionaries and fascist mullahs. Being internationalist it participates in the movements both inside and outside India. It thus fights with the Iranian masses and calls for the overthrow of theological fascism. Similarly it fights for the Kashmir people, the Palestinians, the Kurds, etc. The source of this Revolutionary Internationalism is the dialectic. Truth for this revolutionary dialectic is the "whole", i.e. the world historical revolution.

It is only when this core philosophical question is addressed, only when one understands how the philosophy of praxis can become a realistic program, then and only then, can revolutionary praxis be rendered possible. In this sense the understanding of the dialectic is the core question that is able to analyze the conditions of the possibilities and necessities of the revolution. And that is why we are insisting on calling this revolutionary dialectic (after Gramsci) a historicism and humanism. When one understands this historicism and humanism then authentic left-wing politics realizes itself as the freedom and the will of the radical classes. In this humanist problematic there is no General Secretary that would serve as the vanguard or the destroyer of the revolution.

Dialectics: Point and Counterpoint

At first glance Marx's words: the proletariat "is compelled as proletariat to abolish (*aufzeheben*) itself and thereby its opposite (*Gegensatz*)"[179] not only negates almost all ideas of the Party as we have inherited from the politics of centralism and vanguardism, but also allows the larger and radical inclusive politics of the multitude where caste, oppressed nationalities and gender-democracy form parts of the dialectical whole. It most certainly questions the Stalinist ideas of dictatorships. One must note this dialectic of the *Aufhebung* and *Auflösung* of the proletariat is central to Marx's philosophy of emancipation that was first introduced in the 1843-4 *A Contribution to the Critique of Hegel's Philosophy of Right. Introduction.* Lenin following this humanist Marxist theme talks of "the characterization of dialectics" as "self-movement, the source of all activity, the movement of life and spirit; the coincidence of...humanity with reality..."[180] If one says that in the site of humanist dialectics, the proletariat thus transcends and dissolves itself, then the same ought to be with regard to the caste system. The proletariat and the dalit can only emancipate themselves in this logic of *Aufhebung* and *Auflösung.* Consider Marx:

> Philosophy (of liberation, my insertion, M.J.) cannot realize (*verwirklichen*) itself without the transcendence (*Aufhebung*) of the proletariat, and the proletariat cannot transcend (*aufheben*) itself without the realization (*Verwirklichung*) of philosophy.[181]

What one finds is a difference between this dialectic of liberation and the positivist, instrumental rationality of the Party as the saviour of the working classes. The first is emancipatory, the second despotic. What we will now do is relate this dialectics of *Aufhebung* and *Auflösung* with the radical idea of spontaneity. What the instrumental rationalist (and advocate of some forms of Stalinism and Maoism) does is repudiates this radical idea. After all, so the Stalinists and Maoists claim: "Did Lenin not teach us so?"

But contrary to this positivist and elitist reading (Lenin against spontaneity) we are reading spontaneity in the text of dialectical and historical-humanist materialism. One must stress that one cannot merely define Marxism as dialectical and historical materialism, but as *dialectical and historical-humanist materialism*. It is in this site of communism defined as humanism that one poses the question: Was Lenin against spontaneity? Were then Luxemburg and Trotsky right, and if they were right, were they not also prophetic, for they saw the destructive and authoritarian nature within Lenin's formulation? Or should one read Lenin differently?

This is precisely what we will do. We will read Lenin's *What is to be Done?* in the storm and stress of Kantianism and Hegelianism. Here one will have to insist that despite being burdened with the Kant-Kautsky formulation, Lenin did not repudiate spontaneity as such. What he did was contextualize it in concrete conditions. One knows that one form of spontaneity was that of the economists, who believed in pure trade unionism and the theory of the "inevitable" (*unvermeidliche*) socialist revolution. Like Gramsci's and Lukács' understanding of Marxism as historicism and humanism, Lenin prescribed a theoretical intervention in history. When he said that "without revolutionary theory there can be no revolutionary movement"[182], he implied that only with the most advanced philosophy could the working masses usher in communism.[183] And when he said that the Social Democrats and the economists bowed to spontaneity, he meant that without rigorous theory, they would be enslaved to the fetishism, magic and necromancy of capitalism, that could at will, bring in liberal regimes, fascism, Stalinism and Maoism—all worshipers of the commodity—to crush the masses. Though Lenin did not bring in the ideas of reification and fetishism in the centre of political theory (he was, as we all know unaware of Marx's *Economic and Philosophic Manuscripts of 1844*), he meant that bowing to spontaneity meant bowing to capital accumulation. A professional revolutionary has to be an organic philosopher. The trade unionist is simply useless. Lenin's notion of the vanguard party as the usher of communism and radical democracy is dialectical:

> And so, we have become convinced that the fundamental error committed by the "new trend" of Social-Democracy (Lenin here like all Marxists at that time, meant this to be communism, my insertion, M.J.) is its bowing to spontaneity and its failure to understand that the spontaneity of the masses demands a high degree of consciousness from us Social Democrats. The greater the spontaneous upsurge of the masses and the more widespread the movement, the more rapid, incomparably so, the demand for greater consciousness in the theoretical, political and organizational work of Social-Democracy.[184]

Lenin consequently differentiated spontaneity and spontaneity.[185] In *A Talk with the Defenders of Economism*, Lenin locates a double meaning of spontaneity. Spontaneity is understood in the text of dialectical negation. It is located as *defective* and then *elevated* at the level of consciousness.[186] To elevate means to go through the process of *Aufhebung*—spontaneity is raised at a higher level. What Lenin is doing is displacing the positivist and evolutionist theory of Marxism as being a discourse of estranged laws that exist independent of people. Instead Lenin puts people, consciousness and theory at the centre of Revolutionary Marxism. Lenin here becomes a humanist.

So when one is critiquing the politics of democratic centralism, one ought not to forget this very radical point in Lenin. In differentiating spontaneity as voluntarism, trade unionism and anarchism from the dialectical idea of spontaneity as movement (*Bewegung*) and becoming (*Werden*), Lenin is putting the relation between the party and the masses for theoretical considerations. Those who think that Lenin debunked spontaneity ought to know what he said:

> Movement and "*self-movement*" (this NB! arbitrary (independent), spontaneous, internally-necessary movement), "change",

> "movement and vitality," "the principle of all self-movement,", "impulse" (*Trieb*) to "movement" and to "activity"—the opposite of "*dead Being*"—who would believe that this is the core of "Hegelianism," of abstract and *abstrusen* (ponderous, absurd?) Hegelianism?? This core had to be discovered, understood, *hinuberretten*, laid bare, refined, which is precisely what Marx and Engels did.[187]

Spontaneity as self-movement is now understood as the core of the revolutionary dialectic. This self-movement cannot be willed by consciousness that comes "from the outside". It emerges from within the dialectic process. One should know the difference between the dialectical view of history (motion is within the historical context) and the non-dialectical point of view (motion is brought from the outside: from a "first cause" a "self-caused cause"—which was once understood as a kitsch between the Vedic and Biblical gods).

Conclusion: The Sham Messiah

Any intelligent person would know that the elementary form of all dialectics is the dialectics of combination that forms the leitmotiv of radical politics. One thus combines various forms of struggles. If one has read liberalism as a sham it is because it has within it the bases of inequality between capital and labour. Here this statement makes sense. But if one uses liberalism as sham in the abstract and messianic sense then one would be accompanying, if not the fascist debunking of liberalism, then most certainly the neo-conservative type as exemplified by the Hindutvavadis, neo-cons and the ruling theological regime in contemporary Iran. For the Hindutvavadis, neo-cons and the mullahs, liberalism is indeed sham, just as for the Maoists, parliamentary democracy is sham. One only needs to tell the Maoists, who till very recently called themselves Marxist Leninists, that once-upon-a-time, not long ago, there was a group of ultra-leftists within the Bolsheviks (*Otzovists*, or the 'Boycotters') who refused to work in legal organizations. To the same once-upon-a-time Marxist Leninists, one needs to tell them that Lenin had devoted to them (i.e. to the messiahs in the Communist Movement) an entire text—*'Left-Wing' Communism: An Infantile Disorder*.

Again to the Maoists who are acting more as born-again anarchists with the myth of heroic sacrifice stamped on its banners, one needs to recollect Engels' introduction to Marx's *Class Struggles in France* where he mentions: "the time of surprise attacks, or revolutions carried out by small conscious minorities at the head of the unconscious masses is past".[188]

But then the central Leninist question rings out gain: "What should be done?" Should one say that universal suffrage parallels the Marxist idea of the *Aufhebung* of the state and Engels' withering away of the state? In this sense the revolutionary dictatorship of the proletariat needs to be rethought. Most certainly it is not a return of the old state machinery (bureaucracy, standing army, police, courts, etc.). So what does this power of labour in the dissolution of capital and the state (the guardians of capital) do? It "breaks the modern State power".[189] It forms universal suffrage "to serve the people constituted in Communes".[190] Recall again the idea of *Auflösung*:

> The content of the revolution is the destruction of the instruments of power of the state and their dislodgement (*Auflösung*) with the aid of the power of the proletariat....The struggle ceases only when, as the end result of it, the state organization is completely destroyed.[191]

One destroys the state organization as the guardian of class societies. One destroys Monsieur Capital as the idealized ghost and transcendental essence. In doing so, one also remembers to destroy patriarchy and the narratives supporting it, Biblical or otherwise, on the damnation of women for biting the fruit from the forbidden tree. One remembers likewise to be a humanist through and through. One frees Adam from the spectacle of guilt. Adam stops believing that Monsieur Capital can convert everyone into a bourgeois, making a world after its own terrible capitalist and imperialist image. If theology made up the myth of the forbidden tree where fruits that the peasants and proletariat produced could not be consumed by the multitude, then the New Militants claim that they will destroy this bourgeois tree of the production of surplus value where production is monopolized by the imperialist cartels. These New Militants reverse the nursery tales of the theological 'Fall', where humanity is condemned to the brutal rule of the dictatorship of a terrible and wrathful god. In uprooting the tree of class societies, the New Militants do not create substitute gods, do not create "politics in command" where either the gods (the Stalinists), or the god-men (the Maoists) can usurp human freedom. Instead Marx's song of the "union (*Verein*) of free people"[192] realized as the "free association of moral human beings"[193] drowns the ugly cacophony of the duplicate gods and god-men. This song of free individuals is also realized as the Leninist "direct initiative of the people from below".[194]

One should stress that if one escapes from one end of the binary pole governing contemporary politics (parliamentary politics), then one cannot affirm the other half of the binary (anarcho-terrorism that the Maoists are playing by wearing the mask of the Red Specter). To think dialectically is to think in terms of transcendence-sublation (*Aufhebung*). One then is able to look beyond the avenues of class societies. Marx's idea of species being (*Gattungswesen*) realized as the public sphere (*Öffenlichkeit*) is the name of this new avenue.

Give up the essence of Marxism, give up the masses, humanism and internationalism; and the specters of fascism, neo-conservatism and Stalinism will strike back. Instead of democracy one will have the inquisition and anarchism, not to forget imperialism and occupation. The psychotic will return once again, accompanied by the duplicates, the doubles and the counterfeits.

Is anyone listening?

REFERENCES

1. M.S. Golwalkar, *We, or, Our Nation Defined* (Nagpur, 1947).
2. B.R. Ambedkar, 'Reply to the Mahatma', in Valerian Rodrigues (ed.), *The Essential Writings of B.R. Ambedkar* (New Delhi: Oxford University Press, 2008), p. 317.
3. See B.R. Ambedkar 'Buddha or Karl Marx', in Ibid., p. 178
4. Karl Marx, *Capital*, Vol. I (Moscow: Progress Publishers, 1983), p. 20
5. Karl Marx, 'Communism and the Ausburg *Allgemeine Zeitung*', in *Marx. Engels. Collected Works*, Vol. 1 (Moscow: Progress Publishers, 1975), p. 220. See also Aristotle, *Metaphysics*, Book I, Ch 2, p. 992.
6. Fredric Jameson, *Postmodernism, or, the Cultural Logic of Late Capitalism* (Durham: Duke University Press, 1991), p. 441.
7. Maurice Merleau-Ponty, *Humanism and Terror: An Essay on the Communist Problem* (Boston: Beacon Press, 1990).
8. Leon Trotsky, 'The Case of Leon Trotsky', in *The Basic Writings of Leon Trotsky*, (ed.) Irving Howe (London: Mercury Books, 1964).
9. See her *Women's Liberation and the Dialectics of Revolution. Reaching for the Future* (Detroit: Wayne State University Press, 1996). Also see her *Philosophy and Revolution* (New Jersey: Humanities Press, 1981), *Rosa Luxemburg, Women's Liberation, and Marx's Philosophy of Revolution* (Urbana and Chicago: University of Illinois Press, 1991) and *The Power of Negativity. Selected Writings on the Dialectic of Hegel and Marx*, ed. Peter Hudis and Kevin Anderson (Maryland: Lexington Books, 2002).
10. See his *Lenin, Hegel, and Western Marxism. A Critical Study* (Urbana and Chicago: University of Illinois Press, 1995).
11. Walter Benjamin, 'Edward Fuchs. Collector and Historian', in *One Way Street*, trans. Edmund Jephocott and Kingsley Shorter (London: New Left Books, 1979), p. 265 and my 'On Understanding the Decline of the Established Indian Left', in *Economic and Political Weekly*, June 16, 2012, Vol. XLVII, No. 24, p. 51.
12. Karl Marx, 'Contribution to the Critique of Hegel's Doctrine of the State', in *Karl Marx. Early Writings*, trans. Rodney Livingstone and Gregor Benton (New York: Vintage Books, 1975), p. 62; 'Kritik der Hegelschen Staatsphilosophie' in *Karl Marx. Die Frühschriften* (Stuttgart: Alfred Kröner Verlag, 1964), p. 245.
13. Ibid.
14. Karl Marx, 'To Engels in Manchester, London, January 14, 1858', in *Marx. Engels. Selected Correspondence* (Moscow: Progress

Publishers, 1975), p. 93. Karl Marx, *Das Kapital*, Erster Band (Berlin: Dietz Verlag, 1981), p. 27.

15. Frederick Engels, 'Ludwig Feuerbach and the End of Classical German Philosophy', in *Marx. Engels. Selected Works* (Moscow: Progress Publishers, 1975), p. 591.
16. Karl Marx, *Capital*, Vol. I, p. 29.
17. Ibid., p. 76.
18. Ernst Bloc, *The Principle of Hope*, trans. Neville Plaice, Stephen Plaice and Paul Knight (Oxford: Basil Blackwell. 1986), p. 1354.
19. Karl Marx and Frederick Engels, 'Manifesto of the Communist Party', in *Marx. Engels. Selected Works*, p. 57.
20. Ibid., p. 60.
21. Ibid., p. 54.
22. Ibid, p. 61.
23. Ibid.
24. Karl Marx and Frederick Engels, *The German Ideology* (Moscow: Progress Publishers, 1976), p. 54.
25. Frederick Engels, *Anti-Dühring* (Moscow: Progress Publishers, 1978), pp. 376-7.
26. See Slavoj Žižek, 'A Plea for Leninist Intolerance' in *Critical Inquiry*, Winter, 2002.
27. Slavoj Žižek, 'Postface. Georg Lukács as the Philosopher of Leninism', in Georg Lukács, *A Defence of History and Class Consciousness*, trans. Esther Leslie (London: Verso, 2000), pp. 156-7.
28. Karl Marx, *Economic and Philosophic Manuscripts of 1844* (Moscow: Progress Publishers, 1982), p. 88.
29. Karl Marx, *Capital*, Vol. I, p. 19.
30. Karl Marx and Frederick Engels, *The Holy Family* (Moscow: Progress Publishers, 1980), p. 116. See also my *The Seductions of Karl Marx* (Delhi: Aakar Books, 2010), p. 71.
31. Karl Marx, *Das Kapital*, Erster Band (Berlin: Dietz Verlag, 1981), p. 12.
32. Karl Marx, *Theories of Surplus Value*, Part I (Moscow: Progress Publishers, 1975), p. 40.
33. Karl Marx, *Grundrisse*, trans. Martin Nicolaus (London: Penguin, 1974), p. 100.
34. Karl Marx, *Capital*, Vol. I, p. 19.
35. Frederick Engels, 'To J. Bloch in Königsberg, London, September 21, 1890', in *Marx. Engels. Selected Works* (Moscow: Progress Publishers, 1975), pp. 682-3.
36. Karl Marx, *Capital*, Vol. I, p. 19.

37. Karl Marx, 'To the Editorial Board of the *Otechestvennye Zapiski*, London, November, 1877', in *Marx. Engels. Selected Correspondence* (Moscow: Progress Publishers, 1975), p. 293.
38. Ibid.
39. Karl Marx, 'To J.B. Schweitzer, London, January 24, 1865', in *Marx. Engels. Selected Correspondence* (Moscow: Progress Publishers, 1975), p. 145.
40. Ibid.
41. Louis Althusser, *Lenin and Philosophy*, trans. Ben Brewster (London: New Left Books, 1971), pp. 15-6.
42. Karl Marx, 'To John Baptist Schweitzer, London, January 24, 1865', in *Marx. Engels. Selected Correspondence* (Moscow: Progress Publishers, 1975), pp. 144-5.
43. Karl Marx, *Economic and Philosophic Manuscripts of 1844*, p. 99.
44. Ibid., p. 91.
45. Slavoj Žižek, *The Ticklish Subject* (London: Verso, 1999), p. 139.
46. Karl Marx, 'To Engels, 1853', in *Marx. Engels. Selected Works* (Moscow: Progress Publishers, 1975), pp. 79-80.
47. *Rg Veda, Sacred Writings. Hinduism*, trans. Ralph T.F. Griffith (New York: Quality Paperback Books, 1992), p. 603.
48. See his *The Culture and Civilization of Ancient India in Historical Outline* (New Delhi: Vikas Publishing House, 2000), p. 50.
49. We are keeping this term 'Hinduism' in what Edmund Husserl called "brackets", since we intend to unleash the radical politics of suspicion on this very term that we claim is vacuous and fuzzy.
50. The cultural and economical subordination of the dalits emerges from this Indian form of racism.
51. Leon Trotsky, '1905', in *The Basic Writings of Leon Trotsky*, (ed.) Irving Howe (London: Mercury Books, 1964).
52. Savitri Devi, *Warning to the Hindus* (Calcutta: Hindu Mission, 1939), p. 142.
53. V.I. Lenin, *What is to be Done?* (Moscow: Progress Publishers, 1978), p. 69.
54. See Braj Mani, *De-Brahmanising History* (New Delhi: Manohar, 2011), p. 13.
55. *The Bhagavad Gita*, trans. Swami Chidbhavanda (Tirupparatturai: Tapovanan Publishing House, 1965), p. 109.
56. Karl Marx, 'A Contribution to the Critique of Hegel's Philosophy of Right. Introduction'. In *Karl Marx. Early Writings*, trans. Rodney Livingstone and Gregor Benton (New York: Vintage Books, 1975), p. 243.

57. See Ashis Nandy, 'An Anti-secular Manifesto', in *Seminar*, No. 314, Oct. 1985.
58. Karl Marx, 'The British Rule in India', in *On Colonialism* (Moscow: Progress Publishers, 1976), pp. 40-41.
59. See my 'In Defence of Marxism: A Reply to a Neo-Hindu's Reading of *The Seductions of Karl Marx*', in *Critique*, Vol. 40, No. 1, February 2012, p. 109. See also my *The Legacy of Karl Marx* (Centre for Scientific Socialism, Nagarjuna University, 2012), pp. 56-7.
60. See Aijaz Ahmad, *In Theory. Classes, Nations, Literatures* (New Delhi: Oxford University Press, 1994), p. 224.
61. Ibid., p. 225.
62. Ibid.
63. Karl Marx, 'The British Rule in India', in *On Colonialism* (Moscow: Progress Publishers, 1976), p. 40; and Marx, 'To Engels in Manchester, London, June 14, 1853', in *Marx. Engels. Selected Correspondence* (Moscow: Progress Publishers, 1975), p. 80.
64. Karl Marx, 'The British Rule in India', p. 41.
65. Karl Marx, 'The Future Results of the British Rule in India', in *On Colonialism* (Moscow: Progress Publishers, 1976), p. 81.
66. Karl Marx, *Capital*, Vol. I, p. 20.
67. Karl Marx, *Economic and Philosophic Manuscripts of 1844*, p. 91.
68. Christophe Jaffrelot, *India's Silent Revolution. The Rise of the Low Castes in North Indian Politics* (Delhi: Permanent Black, 2003), pp. 11-2.
69. Ibid.; pp. 13-47.
70. B.R. Ambedkar, 'Gandhism', in *The Essential Writings of B.R. Ambedkar*, ed. Valerian Rodrigues (New Delhi: Oxford University Press, 2008), p. 165.
71. The idea of 'purity' and the construction of a hierarchical social system is not a construction in the void, independent of an economic system. Instead, as Irfan Habib claims: "Concepts of 'purity' and 'pollution' were a rationalization of this basic economic fact". See Irfan Habib, 'Caste in Indian History', in *Essays in Indian History. Towards a Marxist Perception* (New Delhi: Tulika, 1995), p. 166.
72. Irfan Habib, 'Caste in Indian History', p. 166.
73. The Brahmans besides being priests are also scholars and ideologists, not to forget the interpreters of Dharma (the Hindu moral law).
74. The cutting of is evident since the foundational myth in the *Rg Veda, Sacred Writings. Hinduism,* trans. Ralph T.F. Griffith (New York: Quality Paperback Books, 1992), p. 603.

75. Leon Trotsky in *The Permanent Revolution & Results and Prospects* (Delhi: Aakar Books: 2005), p. 40 and in *The Revolution Betrayed* (Delhi: Aakar Books, 2006), pp. 102, 214, 256, links caste as a ossified group with an entrenched closed mentality to the Stalinist bureaucracy.
76. See Irfan Habib, 'Caste in Indian History', in *Essays in Indian History. Towards a Marxist Perception*, p. 169.
77. Ibid., p. 164.
78. Ibid., p. 169.
79. Ibid., p. 173.
80. Ibid., p. 176.
81. Gherardo Gnoli, *Zoroaster's Time and Homeland. A Study on the Origins of Mazdeism and Related Problems* (Naples: Insitituto Universitario Orientale, 1980), p. 186.
82. Albêrûnî, *India. An Account of the Religion, Philosophy, Literature, Geography, Chronology, Laws and Astrology of India about A.D. 1030* (New Delhi: Rupa, 2002), p. 83.
83. The question whether they were originally three or four layers of stratification is hotly debated. See B.R. Ambedkar, *Who were the Shudras?* where he claimed that they were originally three castes and not four.
84. Firdausi, *Sháhnáma*, Vol. I, trans. George Warner and Edmund Warner (London: Kegan Paul, 1915), pp. 132-3.
85. See 'The Gathas of Zarathushtra', in *The Religion of Zarathushtra*, trans. I.J.S. Taraporewala (Bombay: B.I. Taraporewala, 1979), Y. 32.8, p. 155.
86. See *Rg Veda*, Hymn X, 13, p. 535.
87. Jawaharlal Nehru, *The Discovery of India* (New Delhi: Oxford University Press, 1985). See also Perry Anderson, *The Indian Ideology* (New Delhi: Three Essays Collective, 2012).
88. Karl Marx, 'The British Rule in India', in *On Colonialism* (Moscow: Progress Publishers, 1976), pp. 40-41.
89. B.R. Ambedkar, 'Krishna and His Gita', in *The Essential Writings of B.R. Ambedkar*, p. 193.
90. Ibid.
91. Ibid., pp. 195-7.
92. Fredric Jameson, *Postmodernism or the Cultural Logic of Late Capitalism* (London: Verso, 1991), p. 14.
93. Ibid.
94. Ibid.
95. Ibid.

96. Karl Marx and Frederick Engels, *The Holy Family* (Moscow: Progress Publishers, 1980), p. 46.
97. See G.T. Miasnikov, 'To Lenin, 1921', in Paul Avrich, 'Bolshevik Opposition to Lenin: G.T. Miasnikov and the Workers' Group', in *Russian Review*, Vol. 43, 1984. See also Maurice Brinton, *Factory Councils, Soviets, Trade Unions & the Bolshevik Party. 1917-1921* (Nagpur: Spartacus Publication, 1992). Laclau would be a part of the philosophical exponent of post modern anti-Leninism. Contrary to this domain of anti-Leninism, one call recall Slavoj Žižek's 'Have Michael Hardt and Antonio Negri Rewritten the Communist Manifesto for the Twenty-First Century?, in *Rethinking Marxism*, Vol. 13, 3/4 2001.
98. Antonio Negri, *Thirty-Three Lessons on Lenin* (Columbia: Columbia University Press, 2009). Also see Negri, 'Lesson Number One. From the Factory Strategy: 33. Lessons on Lenin: For a Marxist Reading of Lenin's Marxism', in http.// antonionegriinenglish.wordpress.com/24/1/2013.
99. Karl Marx, 'Preface', *A Contribution to the Critique of Political Economy* (Moscow: Progress Publishers, 1978), p. 22.
100. Kevin Anderson, *Lenin, Hegel, and Western Marxism. A Critical Study*, p. 6.
101. V.I. Lenin, *What is to be Done?* pp. 69, 79, 81-2, 85-7, 96, 125-6, 172.
102. Frederick Engels, 'To Franz Mehring in Berlin', p. 690.
103. V.I. Lenin, *Materialism and Empiro-criticism* (Moscow: Progress Publishers, 1977), p. 320.
104. William Shakespeare, 'Julius Caesar', In *The Complete Works of William Shakespeare* (London: Henry Pordes, 1983), Act I, Sc II, p. 890.
105. Karl Marx and Frederick Engels, 'Manifesto of the Communist Party', p. 53.
106. Karl Korsch, 'Leninism and the Comintern', in Douglas Kellner, *Karl Korsch. Revolutionary Theory* (Austin & London: University of Texas Press, 1977), p. 152.
107. Karl Marx, *Das Kapital*, Erster Band, p. 88.
108. Slavoj Žižek, *The Sublime Object of Ideology* (London: Verso, 1989), p. 29.
109. See my 'Leninism as Radical Desireology' in *Economic and Political Weekly*, September 24, 2011, Vol. XLVI, No. 39.
110. Rosa Luxemburg, 'Organizational Questions of Social Democracy', in *Rosa Luxemburg. Selected Writings* (Kolkata: Search, 2008), p. 117.

111. Ibid.
112. Here I disagree with Žižek's formulation of the party where the party is considered as the individual. See his 'Postface', p. 159.
113. Once again one disagrees with Žižek's formulation of the party as the mediator between history and the proletariat.
114. Frederick Engels, 'The Condition of England. I. The Eighteenth Century' in *Marx. Engels. Collected Works,* Vol. 3 (Moscow: Progress Publishers, 1975).
115. Karl Marx, *Capital,* Vol. I, p. 77.
116. Karl Marx, *Capital,* Vol. III, (Moscow: Progress Publishers, 1986), p. 830.
117. Ibid.
118. Karl Marx, *Economic and Philosophic Manuscripts of 1844,* p. 110.
119. Karl Marx, *Das Kapital,* Ertser Band, (Berlin: Dietz Verlag, 1981), p. 52.
120. Sigmund Freud, 'The Uncanny', in *Sigmund Freud Vol. 14. Art and Literature* (London: Penguin, 1985), p. 339.
121. Ibid., p. 340.
122. Ibid.
123. Ibid., pp. 341-2.
124. Ibid., pp. 342, 346.
125. Ibid.
126. Ibid., p. 347.
127. Ibid., p. 350.
128. Karl Marx, 'Theses on Feuerbach", in *Marx. Engels. Selected Works,* (Moscow: Progress Publishers, 1975), p. 28.
129. Ibid.
130. Ibid.
131. Johann Wolfgang Goethe, *Faust,* Part I, trans. Philip Wayne (London: Penguin, 1949), p. 67.
132. Karl Marx, *Theories of Surplus Value,* Part I (Moscow: Progress Publishers, 1975), p. 390
133. Max Horkheimer, *Eclipse of Reason* (London: Continuum, 2004), pp. 78-9.
134. William Shakespeare, 'Hamlet', Act I, Sc. V, p. 948.
135. Ibid., p. 946.
136. Ibid., Act I, Sc V, p. 948.
137. Fyodor Dostoevsky, *Crime and Punishment* (Moscow: Ruduga Publishers, 1985), p. 280.
138. Walter Benjamin, 'Theses on the Philosophy of History', in *Illuminations,* (London: Fontana/Collins, 1979), p. 264. Also see

Antonio Negri, *Time for Revolution* (London: Continuum, 2003), p. 106.

139. Walter Benjamin, op. cit.
140. As quoted in Dilip Simeon, *Revolutionary Highways* (New Delhi: Penguin, 2010), p. 87.
141. Johann Wolfgang Goethe, *Faust*, Part I, trans. Philip Wayne (London: Penguin, 1949), p. 48.
142. Ibid., p. 71.
143. Karl Marx, *Capital*, Vol. I, p. 90.
144. Karl Marx, 'Review of Chenu's *les Conspirateur's. Par A. Chenu, Ex-capitaine des Gardes Du Citoyen Caussidiére. Les Sociétés Secrétes'*, in *Marx. Engels. Collected Works*, Vol. 10 (Moscow: Progress Publishers, 1978), p. 319.
145. Walter Benjamin, op. cit., p. 265.
146. Ibid.
147. Ibid.
148. William Shakespeare, 'Hamlet', Act I, Sc. IV. p. 949.
149. Karl Marx and Frederick Engels, 'Manifesto of the Communist Party', in *Marx. Engels. Selected Works* (Moscow: Progress Publishers, 1975), p. 35.
150. Ibid.
151. Karl Marx, *Economic and Philosophic Manuscripts of 1844*, pp. 135-6.
152. Ibid., p. 136.
153. Ibid., pp. 96, 111, 136.
154. Ibid., p. 120.
155. Slavoj Žižek, 'Lenin's Choice: Interpretation vs. Formalization' in www.Lacan.com. 24-1-2013.
156. See my *The Legacy of Karl Marx* (Centre for Scientific Socialism: Acharya Nagarjuna University, 2012).
157. Slavoj Žižek, 'A Plea for Leninist Intolerance', in *Critical Inquiry*, Winter, 2002.
158. V.I. Lenin, *What is to be Done?* (Moscow: Progress Publishers, 1978), p. 26.
159. Slavoj Žižek, 'A Plea for Leninist Intolerance'.
160. Frederick Engels, 'To Franz Mehring in Berlin, London, July 14, 1893', in *Marx. Engels. Selected Works* (Moscow: Progress Publishers, 1975), p. 690.
161. See Slavoj Žižek, 'Seize the Day: Lenin's Legacy'.
162. Karl Marx, *Economic and Philosophic Manuscripts of 1844*, p. 120.
163. Quoted in Georg Lukács, *Lenin. A Study on the Unity of his Thought* (Cambridge, Massachusetts: The MIT Press, 1974) p. 94.

164. Ibid.
165. See my 'Leninism as Radical Desireology', in *Economic and Political Weekly*, Vol. XLVI, No. 39, Sept. 24, 2011.
166. Ibid., p. 20.
167. V.I. Lenin, 'State and Revolution', in *Lenin, Selected Works* (Moscow: Progress Publishers, 1977), pp. 293, 297.
168. Karl Marx and Frederick Engels, *The German Ideology* (Moscow: Progress Publishers, 1976), p. 42; 'Die deutsche Ideologie', *Karl Marx. Die Frühschriften* (Stuttgart: Alfred Kröner Verlag, 1964), p. 349.
169. G.W.F. Hegel, *Science of Logic*, trans. A.V. Miller (London: George Allen & Unwin, 1969), p. 107.
170. Karl Marx, 'On the Jewish Question', in *Karl Marx. Early Writings*, trans. Rodney Livingstone and Gregor Benton, p. 216.
171. Ibid.
172. Karl Marx, 'A Contribution to the Critique of Hegel's Philosophy of Right. Introduction', in *Karl Marx. Early Writings*, p. 244.
173. Karl Marx, *Economic and Philosophic Manuscripts of 1844*, p. 91.
174. Karl Marx and Frederick Engels, 'Die deutsche Ideologie', in *Die Frühschriften*, p. 367.
175. Karl Marx and Frederick Engels, *The German Ideology*, p. 54.
176. Karl Marx, 'Nationalökonomie und Philosophie', in *Die Frühschriften*, p. 235.
177. From this little note on the question of the dialectic we have noted that three sites have to be transcended—alienation, private property and the state. Later, as we all very well know, Marx talked of the smashing of the state, a theme that Lenin had kept at the centre of his *State and Revolution*, a theme that the parliamentary left has simply forgotten.
178. Karl Marx, *Economic and Philosophic Manuscripts of 1844*, pp. 90, 91, 94, 109, 132, 143; 'Nationalökonomie und Philosophie', in *Die Frühschriften*, pp. 251, 264, 271, 280-82.
179. Karl Marx and Frederick Engels, *The Holy Family* (Moscow: Progress Publishers, 1980), p. 46.
180. V.I. Lenin, *Philosophical Notebooks, Collected Works*. Vol. 38 (Moscow: Progress Publishers, 1980), p. 228.
181. Karl Marx, 'A Contribution to the Critique of Hegel's Philosophy of Right. Introduction', p. 257.
182. V.I. Lenin, *What is to be Done?*, p. 25.
183. Ibid., p. 26.
184. Ibid., p. 53.
185. Ibid., p. 31.

186. V.I. Lenin, 'A Talk with the Defenders of Economism', in *Lenin. Selected Works*, p. 46.
187. V.I. Lenin, *Philosophical Notebooks, Collected Works*. Vol. 38 (Moscow: Progress Publishers, 1980), p. 141.
188. Frederick Engels, 'Introduction to Marx's Class Struggles in France', in *Marx. Engels. Selected Works in Three Volumes*, Vol. 2 (Moscow: Progress Publishers, 1977), p. 200.
189. Karl Marx, 'The Civil War in France', in *Marx. Engels. Selected Works*, p. 289.
190. Ibid.
191. V.I. Lenin, 'State and Revolution', in *Lenin. Selected Works*, p. 342.
192. Karl Marx, *Capital*, Vol. I, p. 82.
193. Karl Marx, 'The Leading Article in No. 179 of the *Kölinische Zeitung*', in *Marx. Engels. Collected Works*, Vol. 1 (Moscow: Progress Publishers, 1975), pp. 192-3.
194. V.I. Lenin, 'The Dual Power', in *V.I. Lenin. Selected Works in Three Volumes*, Vol. 2 (Moscow: Progress Publishers, 1977), p. 34.